D0647976

Librarians as Professionals

Librarians as Professionals

The Occupation's Impact on Library Work Arrangements

William Joseph Reeves
The University of Calgary

LexingtonBooks
D.C. Heath and Company
Lexington, Massachusetts
Toronto

Library of Congress Cataloging in Publication Data

Reeves, William Joseph
    Librarians as professionals.

    Bibliography: p.
    Includes index.
    1. Librarians. 2. Library administration. I. Title.
Z682.R35   020'.23   79-2389
ISBN 0-669-03163-1

Published simultaneously in Canada

Printed in the United States of America

International Standard Book Number: 0-669-03163-1

Library of Congress Catalog Card Number: 79-2389

To Myrna

Contents

Contents

List of Figures

List of Tables

Preface

It seems a long time ago, in 1972, that I first turned my attention to this topic. I was struck by the seemingly ubiquitous uniformities displayed by formal organizations. At the time I was intrigued by the ease with which a friend of mine from Alberta, Canada, entered the school system in Sydney, Australia. His competence as a teacher was almost instantaneously affirmed upon his arrival, even though he was trained in Alberta and was all but uninformed about Australia or its system of education. I suspected that this capacity to transpose occupational skills and work arrangements from one organizational context to another was in some fashion part of the symmetry I had noted in formal organizations. I realized that current theory in the field of occupations or organizations did not provide satisfactory accounts of these phenomena, and my hunches were largely supported by my subsequent research. However, I am now taken aback by my confidence in starting this project, given that the literature provided little or no guidance.

I would like to acknowledge the people who have helped me through the years. My initial ideas took form while at Stanford University during informal discussions with Dick Scott, Rick Rubinson, John Meyer, and Franzie Cancian. After moving to the University of Calgary, I made little progress until I had the fortune to talk with librarians at the university library. Their interest and support enabled me to convert my tentative thoughts into a concrete research project. As my fieldwork progressed from exploratory interviews to pretests into the survey itself, I found that my experiences at the university were duplicated throughout the Province of Alberta. The courtesy and cooperation extended to me by those that I interviewed were most rewarding experiences. My dismay at the volume and apparent ambiguity of my results was dispelled by some timely advice on editing techniques from Sandy Labovitz. It was on the basis of his succinct maxims that I began to educate myself in the art of sifting results for findings. Toward the end, Dick Scott, John Meyer, and Jim Frideres gave me the advice and moral support that sustained me.

Over the past seven years the help that I have received at critical times from friends and colleagues has made it possible for me to continue. Even more important, the patience and support of Myrna Kutzi-Reeves made it possible for this project to come to a successful conclusion.

Introduction

There is a paradoxical relationship between the standards of librarianship and library service established by library associations, on the one hand, and conditions of work as they exist in most libraries, on the other. Like many other technical and semiprofessionals, librarians possess normative standards that define how work is to be done but lack the legal authority and economic power of the established professions to enforce those standards on the job. Library associations establish goals for library service knowing that existing guidelines are ignored in many libraries. Librarians, imbued with the principles of librarianship while in training, may abandon these precepts in practice. That there is any connection between theory and practice is a wonder. Is there any use in formulating policies that cannot be enforced? The findings of this study suggest that there is. The resolutions passed by library associations appear to have an impact on work arrangements in some libraries, but only under certain circumstances and conditions. In exploring the relationship between theory and practice, we shall find it necessary to revise some of our ideas about the nature of professionalism, organizational administration, and occupational authority in organizational settings.

This study combined a survey of the policies published by library associations with a survey of library work settings. The objective was to identify circumstances and conditions that fostered occupational control over work in organizational settings. The key discovery was that the occupational authority of the librarian depended on the orientations of others in the library work setting—on the collective orientations of nonlibrarians as well as librarians on the staff. The personal orientations of the librarian were relevant only insofar as they were reinforced by the collective sentiments of others. In work settings collectively oriented toward library associations, work arrangements tended to conform to standards articulated by those associations. The greater the collective occupational orientations, the closer the relationship between practice and policy. In the system of library administration prescribed by library associations, librarians are legitimated as the dominant occupation in library work settings. The collective occupational orientations of others in the work setting appeared to determine whether librarians assumed the rights and responsibilities of leadership as defined by their occupation, and whether they were in a position to institute the appropriate occupational system of library operations. The enforcement of occupational standards depended on normative orientations within the work setting and not on the legal and economic power of the occupation in the larger society.

The librarian occupation lacks the structural powers of an established profession. While librarians are corporately organized by library associations and schools, they do not have the right to license practitioners, enforce standards of practice, or enter into contractual negotiations on behalf of librarians. In contrast, the occupation possesses well-defined normative foundations. These policies define the librarian's domain of competence in terms of the tasks involved in providing library service and the occupations that typically work under the direction of the librarian. The standards of these library associations stipulate the appropriate duties for each occupation and the structure of administration that should govern library operations.

The relevance of these policies in a library work setting is hypothesized to depend on the collective occupational orientations of the staff. An inspection of the results of the library survey reveals that there is considerable variation from one library to another in the level of collective occupational orientations. Thus we expect the occupation to influence the structure of work arrangements in only some of the libraries surveyed, in those collectively oriented toward the occupation. Occupational standards have an impact on the use of job descriptions and written records and on the pattern of role expectations and communication in occupationally oriented library settings. Multivariate regression analysis is employed to distinguish the effects associated with occupational orientations from those attributable to nonoccupational factors. (A short explanation of regression analysis appears in the introduction to chapter 6.)

Bureaucratic modes of control in library work settings can be traced to the policies articulated by library associations. Librarians in occupationally oriented settings institute a system of library administration that conforms to library association standards. This system of library administration is denoted by formalized work arrangements and a centralized pattern of communication. These occupationally derived, organizational structures reinforce the librarian's occupational authority and control over work in the library.

In stressing the importance of standards of librarianship and library service to occupational authority, I am proposing that the occupation must furnish an organized body of knowledge, policies, doctrines, or principles that defines how library work does and should proceed. This relationship between occupational ideology outside the work setting and the accepted social definition of the situation within the work setting is central to the analysis of the occupational control over work. What I am not proposing is that we engage in another evaluation of the librarian occupation from the perspective of "the professionalism ideology." Sociologists have run the risk of becoming apologists for the professionalism ideology in attempting to identify the unique attributes that separate professionals from nonprofessionals, and the professions from other occupations and jobs. Roth (1974, p. 7) states that "when we examine each of these . . . attributes, we see that they are largely mixtures of unproven—indeed unexamined—claims for professional control and autonomy." Most authors who have written on the professional status of librarians have accepted the professional ideology and have found, not surprisingly, that librarians have neither the legal and economic rights nor the service orientations of doctors, lawyers, and the clergy. Rather than being concerned with the styles of service and patterns of work that are uniquely professional and then comparing this profile to the policies of library associations, this study researches the styles of service and patterns of work advocated by library associations and compares that profile to actual work arrangements found in a survey of libraries. Thus I am suggesting not only a reevaluation of the roles of normative institutions and structural power vis-à-vis occupational control over work but also a change in the way in which we evaluate the significance of normative institutions to occupational authority.

Part I
The Librarian Occupation

1

Librarians Are Not Professionals: A Conventional Perspective

The people in charge of work settings within libraries, including "media centers, learning centers, educational resource centers, information, documentation, and referral centers" ("Library education," *American Libraries*, 1970, p. 341) are typically regarded as librarians by library users and the public at large. Librarians make up the top line of command in public libraries. In comparison, in many libraries serving governmental agencies and business firms, their line authority is all but eclipsed by their staff functions in the larger organization. Nevertheless, it is their preeminent position in the organization and management of library services that seems to characterize the librarian occupation.

Librarians themselves tend to restrict their conception of the occupation to those who have a baccalaureate in the arts, sciences, or humanities and have undergone postgraduate training in library work. Library associations and the more "professional" members of the occupation are even more discriminating. These associations reserve the title librarian to those who have completed their library training at an accredited library school.

Representative Associations and Schools

In North America library schools came into existence at approximately the same time as library associations. In the United States the first school was organized in 1887, with fifteen in existence by 1919. The American Library Association (ALA) was incorporated earlier than that (1876) but did not publish a journal until 1907. The ALA did not attempt to set standards in the field until 1924. It is likely that the faculty of library schools and their graduates were largely instrumental in shaping these associations during their early period of existence. Perhaps as a result, the ALA proposed to raise the standards in the occupation by accrediting library schools rather than by examining and certifying individual practitioners.[1]

The parallel organization in Canada, the Canadian Library Association (CLA), was not organized until after World War II (1947). At that time, four schools were already in operation in Canada—McGill and Toronto had been operating for over fifteen years. As of 1974 one French-speaking, one bilingual, and six English-speaking universities in Canada offered degrees in library science.[2] Of the schools offering programs in English, Montreal, McGill, Toronto, the University of British, and the University of Western Ontario were accredited by the ALA in 1974, and Dalhousie was accredited in 1976 ("Accreditation of Programs," *American Libraries*, 1970, p. 1092). Most schools had shifted or intended to shift form a one-year postgraduate bachelor of library science (BLS) degree to a two-year master of library science (MLS) degree.[3] In Canada, library schools have always had university affiliation. Active support of the university systems by both the provincial and federal governments ensured that the library schools were not marginal operations, easing the perceived need for accreditation (Bissell, 1974). At the time of its inception, the CLA Council (Canadian Library Association Council, 1947, p. 5) passed the following resolution: "That until such time as the Canadian Library Association can set up its own Board, the Association accepts the accrediting of the Board of Education for Librarianship of the American Library Association." The issue whether to set up a Canadian system has been reconsidered several times since then (1955, 1958, 1965, and 1974-75).[4] Each time the issue has emerged, the status quo favoring the ALA system has been reaffirmed.[5]

The stated aims of library associations reveal dual purposes: to promote the advancement of library service and to promote the advancement of librarianship. This ambiguity is not unintended. Membership in the ALA and the CLA, as well as in most other library associations, is open both to individuals and to organizations "interested in librarianship." The Blau-Scott (1962, pp. 42-57) typology of "who benefits" may be used to identify those who may be interested in librarianship: (1) members of library staff, librarians as well as non-librarians, (2) owner-managers (for example, trustees), (3) the public in contact (for example, library patrons, clients, users), and (4) the public at large (for example, citizens). Some associations will not extend membership to the public at large, restricting membership only to those clients who are organized and who have "interest group" status (for example, the Special Libraries Association). While different classes of membership are often designated, active participation in most, if not all, library associations is not limited to members of the librarian occupation. Their official aims and membership requirements seem to indicate that library associations have a policy of co-opting important groups in their domain. To the extent that librarians continue to dominate the proceedings of these associations, as they seem to be doing, the co-optation would be of a formal rather than of an informal nature (Selznick, 1949, p. 19). Subscribing nonlibrarians seem to be organized as a public responsive to the pronouncements and policies of the associations.

The result of this widespread policy of co-optation is that no clear lines of demarcation separate one library association from another, or the occupation from other interests. Common themes and open membership policies belie the geographical and specialty claims implied by the titles of the associations. Moves to sharpen jurisdictional distinctions between associations do not seem to have occurred or else have been rebuffed. For example, the policy on accreditation is potentially the most salient jurisdictional issue between the ALA and the CLA. However, the CLA has consistently avoided any split from the ALA system, and the ALA has moved to accommodate the interests of the CLA in the accreditation process.[6] The presence of "nonprofessional" members, as well as the attention given to objectives that do not directly further the interests of librarians, has caused some commentators to despair.[7]

An Abstract Body of Knowledge

The existence of an abstract body of knowledge and prolonged training to gain employment have been regarded as characteristics that separate a profession from other occupations and jobs. Professional authority is seen to rest, in part, in the mystique associated with technical expertise and in the capacity to provide a systematic rationale that justifies the imposition of occupational standards of practice. Librarians have not succeeded in establishing control over an esoteric body of knowledge (Boissonnas, 1972; Goode, 1961; North, 1976). The policies and standards articulated by library associations and schools do not have the abstractness and logical rigor associated with the established professions of medicine, law, or theology. More important, librarians control neither creation of nor access to their specialized area of knowledge. Many nonlibrarians including publishers, academics, and specialists in computer-based information systems are as knowledgeable as librarians about sources of information and techniques of information processing. Prolonged, specialized training in this body of knowledge is not even a prerequisite for employment. Librarians are not licensed (Vandergrift, 1978) and may not even be graduates of accredited library programs.[8] The overall pattern that emerges bears a strong resemblance to the strategy of library associations regarding membership and representation: the occupation utilizes the knowledge bases of nonlibrarians, blurs lines of jurisdiction that might distinguish librarians from nonlibrarians, and fails to demarcate a theoretical domain reserved solely for librarians.

Legal Status

The state may endorse occupational institutions by vesting practitioners and their representative associations with the authority to regulate conditions of work or by establishing occupational standards and jurisdiction as legally enforceable rights. Either by collaborating with the state or by utilizing authority delegated by the state, an occupation increases its capacity to enforce its standards of practice. Professions have typically used this authority to require all practitioners to pass minimum standards for entry into an occupation and to conform to a code of ethics in the conduct of their work. Unions as well as professions have been allowed to exercise collective bargaining rights (interpreted in the widest sense of the phrase) in negotiations affecting conditions of employment. By participating in the legislative or executive functions of the state, many occupations have influenced the establishment of relevant regulations.

In North America the sovereign has not endorsed occupational standards for librarians.[9] Perhaps this lack of involvement in the affairs of the occupation is related to the structure of library associations. By and large, library associations have attempted to embrace the interests that populate the markets for librarians and library services—the suppliers and employers of formally trained librarians and the sponsors and consumers of library services. To the extent that library associations have succeeded in co-opting these groups, the apparent need for government regulation of these markets is muted. In most cases the library associations have limited themselves to petitioning the government on issues relating to government sponsorship of libraries and library schools. The associations seem to be unwilling to represent the specific interests of librarians per se or to petition the government to eliminate improprieties and invidious conditions of work.[10]

In the absence of legally vested rights, library associations do not enforce standards of conduct for the members of the occupation. The ALA (but apparently not the CLA) has a code of ethics and a library bill of rights but does not possess the means even to boycott offending libraries or librarians. Attempts by the ALA to regulate entry into the occupation are far from effective.[11] While all library schools in Canada are now accredited by the ALA, the situation is far worse in the United States—only 55 of 120 schools offering programs in library science were accredited in 1971 (Boissonnas, 1972, p. 975). Boissonnas stressed this point when commenting on the ALA's minimum standards for libraries: "ALA calls these 'standards' but, in fact, they are nothing more than recommendations, since there is no mechanism in existence by which they can be enforced" (1972, p. 975).

Market Status

An occupation attains a permanent market status when consensus regarding its task domain is shared by employers as well as by training schools and representative associations (Stinchcombe, 1959, p. 168). Domain consensus makes an occupational career a possibility.[12] Integration of the qualifications awarded by schools with hiring priorities establishes a future for those enrolled in formal training programs. Movement from schools into positions, and from one position to another, structures the market for the types of skills and experience provided by the occupation. A permanent market status stabilizes the task domain of an occupation. Deviation from the predefined packages of personal qualifications and job characteristics of the task domain reduces career opportunities for individuals and creates problems of recruitment for potential employers. By generating conditions in which occupational standards become self-fulfilling prophecies, permanent market status increases the reality of occupational labels and rules of conduct.

In the province of Alberta, Canada, a general consensus regarding the status of the librarian seems to exist among employers, librarians, and library schools and associations. In the survey of libraries conducted in 1974, all forty-six individuals who identified themselves as a librarian had in fact graduated from accredited schools.[13] The person in charge was a librarian in twenty-nine of the thirty-two settings included in the survey. While some employers may not be aware of the qualifications and distinctions stressed by library associations and schools, a specialized, advanced education seemed to be a generally acknowledged prerequisite for employment in the occupation.

The career options available to a librarian are similar to those open to any technically qualified official (Stinchcombe, 1965, p. 165). In addition to moving up the administrative hierarchy within a library, the librarians' educational qualifications enable them to move from one organization to another. Beyond providing these educational qualifications, the occupation has very little impact on the market and conditions of employment. Unlike schools that provide training for some other occupations, library schools have not extended their control into the work setting by administering apprenticeship programs. Library associations have tended to co-opt employers rather than act as bargaining agents for librarians in negotiations with employers. Control over employment—hiring, promotion, and dismissal of librarians and those in ancillary occupations—rests primarily with employers. Librarians who exercise this control do so as employers and not necessarily as members of the librarian occupation.

Conclusions

The occupation is unable to determine who can and who cannot practice as a librarian; it controls neither access into the occupation through the formal avenues of socialization nor entry into positions of employment. Without the capacity to exercise a monopoly over the performance of certain tasks, the occupation cannot achieve the visible and distinctive attributes of status that distinguish a profession. The occupation is unable to make any claim regarding the crucial importance of its skills and knowledge to society and the individual members of society. It is unable to increase the economic well-being and thus the prestige of practitioners. It is unable to command the allegiance of practitioners to a common style of work and life. Whether one emphasizes the exchange power associated with an economic monopoly (Goode, 1957, 1961, 1969) or the sense of mystery and competence derived from a monopoly of knowledge (Berger and Luckman, 1966; Friedson, 1970), library associations have not attained the foundations possessed by a profession.

Notes

1. In a debate with Wilensky (1964), Johnson (1972) has suggested that there is no set sequence in the development of the professional traits of an occupation. He went on to suggest that where associations predated schools, a system of licensing individual practitioners seemed to emerge (corresponding with Wilensky's suggested order of events), but where schools predate the existence of professional associations, a system of accreditation of schools rather than individuals seems to occur. The system of accreditation, first put into place in 1924, has been modified several times since (1933, 1948, 1951, 1956, 1966, 1973). See Summers and Bidlack (1972).

2. These include McGill University (1927), University of Toronto (1928), University of Ottawa (1938, bilingual), University of Montreal (1939, French), University of British Columbia (1961), University of Western Ontario (1967), University of Alberta (1968), and Dalhousie University (1969). See Megrian (1974). The program at the University of Ottawa has since been discontinued.

3. As of 1973 McGill, Toronto, Montreal, Western Ontario, and Dalhousie offered only a two-year MLS. The University of Ottawa (the other nonaccredited school) offered both a BLS and an MLS. The University of British Columbia still only offered a one-year BLS but had endorsed the Canadian Association of Library Schools' norm of a two-year MLS. As of 1976 the University of British Columbia adopted the MLS. The University of Alberta offered both the BLS and the MLS after 1971, dropping the BLS in 1976. In 1970 the ALA adjusted its standards from a one-year BLS to a two-year MLS. Although no grandfather clause was included, the BLS was still recognized as valid for Canada (Megrian, 1974).

4. See Rothstein (1974). See also the entire June 1974 issue of the *Canadian Library Journal* and also "Accreditation—Pro and Con," *Feliciter* (1975).

5. See "Accreditation of Programs," *American Libraries* (1970), for a description of the structure. In 1955 a target date of 1960 was set for consideration of a Canadian system. However, in 1958 the CLA acceptance of ALA accreditation was amended to read "until such time as the situation demands" instead of "until 1960." Here the situation still stands.

6. Rothstein (1974), *Canadian Library Journal* (June 1974), "Accreditation—Pro and Con" (1975).

7. See Bishop (1973) for a pessimistic view. See also Boissonnas (1972, p. 978).

8. The ALA has explicitly denied that one of the purposes of accreditation is to improve the employment situation for librarians. The ALA stated that accreditation should not be denied to schools that meet established standards, nor should these schools be expected to regulate the number of entering students as a condition of regulation. "All accrediting efforts should be developed for the benefit of the public and not primarily the interests of the

professionals or practitioners in the field being accredited" ("Statement on Accreditation and the Employment Situation," *American Libraries* 6 (1975):39.

9. Boissonnas (1972, p. 973). Where licensing of librarians does occur in the United States, certification by the state is entirely unrelated to ALA accreditation.

10. In 1975 the ALA changed its statement of goals to place greater emphasis on political lobbying. ("ALA Goals and Objectives," *American Libraries*, 1975.) Whether the ALA will also move toward representing the occupational interests of librarians and away from representing the dual interests of libraries and librarianship is not clear. In Canada librarians are channeling collective action for employment benefits and rights through local affiliation with labor unions and faculty bargaining units, not through the library associations (Schroeder, 1975).

11. Friedson (1970, p. 94) argues that even the minimal attempt at influence represented by a boycott fails to regulate professional conduct. "This device does not control the boycotted person's behavior so much as it pushes him outside the boundaries of observability and influence, to practice as he wishes in the company of those with similar standards." However, the boycott in monopolistic market conditions is an instrument for raising the status of members in good standing. See also "Statement on Accreditation and the Employment Situation," *American Libraries* 6(1975):39.

12. *Domain consensus* is a phrase coined by Thompson (1967, pp. 28-29).

13. Interviews were completed in thirty-two of a possible thirty-six (89 percent) libraries, learning resource centers, materials centers, and archives in the province of Alberta. See appendix A for a more complete description of the sampling procedures.

2

The Beginning
of a Reappraisal

Librarians work within formal organizations. Thus we must clearly distinguish between occupational authority and its sources from managerial authority. Social control in organizations may be derived from the exercise of line authority or from the application of occupational standards and principles. Parsons (1960, p. 95) expressed objections to "the continuous line-authority picture of formal organizations." At the technical level of organization, he suggested that "it is fundamental to modern society that a large range of its functions are performed in *occupational* roles by persons who have no ascriptive or associational connection with the organization but are *employed* by it through a formal or informal contract of employment" (p. 78). The authority of such persons is derived in large part from sources outside the organization in which they work, from the social and economic foundations of their occupation. These foundations include representative associations and training schools, the institutions or system of rules of conduct articulated by the associations and schools, a market status, and vested rights to participate in the legislation, execution, and adjudication of occupational standards by or on behalf of the state.

The foundations of an occupation include both normative and structural elements. The *normative* order is represented by the beliefs and values articulated by their associations and schools. At the very least, these beliefs and values trace the current position and past history of an occupation (an industrial union). Beyond this, they may constitute an idealized model of operations and procedures to be carried out in the task domain, providing the knowledge base for an occupational technology (a craft union, semiprofession, or profession). Should the associations or schools succeed in incorporating occupational standards into the normative order of the state, the task domain would be extended into and integrated with the central value system of the society.

The *structural* order comprises all behaviors oriented toward the occupational normative order. Occupational structures include any collective action by members of an occupation as well as the actions of associations and schools to enforce existing occupational institutions. By regulating conditions of work and access into the occupation, associations and schools establish the integrity and value of services rendered by the occupation, ensuring a demand for those services. By also regulating access of the public to those services, the structure of the market can be manipulated, creating a source of power for individual members and their representatives. In the terms proposed by Weber (1946, pp. 180-195) an occupation may constitute a party as well as a status group. To the extent that associations and schools are able to establish institutions defining a distinctive style of work, these occupational bodies represent the interests of a status group. To the extent that those same associations or schools attempt to affect the central value system of the larger society, the associations or schools and those that subscribe to their societal actions constitute a party. An occupation would have to take action as a party to successfully limit membership in the group and establish a monopoly.[1] The occupation's institutions make up its normative foundations; its market and legal statuses form its structural foundations.[2] The positions held by members of an occupation are part of a much larger occupational order, a system that extends beyond the immediate work setting in which those positions may exist.

According to the conventional perspective, the perspective used to evaluate the librarian occupation, the ability of the individual members of an occupation to have control over their work is traced to the collective, structurally based power of their occupation. Authority within a work setting is predicated on the acceptance of the occupation's sphere of competence by organized interests outside the work setting (Friedson, 1970; Goode, 1957). Occupational associations, often acting in conjunction with the state, enforce occupational standards. Faced with opposition that interferes with occupational duties, an individual practitioner may appeal outside the work setting for support from his occupation. The power of occupational associations to launch successful collective or legal actions on behalf of individual members is generally contingent on the occupation's possessing a market monopoly, a monopoly over learning structures or a legal monopoly over the performance of certain tasks.[3] Agreement on the task domain signaled by widespread compliance by employers and by the backing of the state legitimizes occupational standards and practices. From a structural perspective, both the power and the legitimacy of individual practitioners are derived from sources outside their work settings. The occupational authority of individual members is directly related to the power of their occupation to enforce occupational standards. Within work settings authority is imputed to practitioners in recognition of the structural foundations of their occupation outside the setting.

A corollary of this argument is that such authority is not imputed to members of an occupation that lacks well-established structural foundations. For example, occupational authority should not be imputed to a librarian because the librarian occupation is not structually powerful. The validity of such a conclusion is questioned. Rather, from the perspective of this study, occupational authority in a work setting rests on the normative and not necessarily on the structural foundations of an occupation. Because library associations and schools lack the power to enforce their standards, the settings in which librarians work may or may not be oriented toward these occupational norms. However, in occupationally oriented settings, librarians draw authority from their occupational status and are in a position to institute an appropriate system of library administration. The power to control library work arrangements is derived from the collective occupational orientations of others in the work setting. Collective occupational orientations indicate that there is an appearance of unanimous acceptance of occupational standards by nonlibrarians as well as librarians and that relationships of status superiority and inferiority are modeled on those occupational institutions. Librarians may rely on the endorsement of others to enforce occupational work arrangements. By justifying their administration in terms of the standards of library service, librarians legitimate their control over work. The authority of the librarian emanates from the normative standards established by library associations and schools and from normative orientations toward those standards in the work setting. It does not necessarily depend on the library associations having the structural power to enforce standards of librarianship.

Figure 2-1 illustrates the interaction between the normative and structural foundations of an occupation. For simplicity, the interaction is presented as a two-by-two table, dichotomizing each dimension into only two values—high or low. Of course, occupations may vary between these extremes. Positions in cell 1 are generally organized by management. In the absence of structural as well as normative foundations outside the immediate organizational work setting, management can reconstitute or eliminate such positions at will. Generally, these positions are called jobs rather than occupations; individual workers do not enjoy any sense of occupational authority on the job.

Unionized jobs (cell 2) have legally vested bargaining rights and often enjoy a market monopoly. However, industrial unions typically have not gone beyond defining their occupational jurisdiction to articulate an occupationally based technology. Social commentators have noted that many if not most industrial unions in Western Europe and North America have concentrated on the economic welfare of their members, trading off control over work arrangements for increases in wages and fringe benefits. (See Mann, 1973, for a summary of this perspective.) Members of such unions have a veto power over job reclassifications or reorganizations proposed by management. These rights constitute a minimal and truncated form of occupational authority.

Many industrial unions approach the established professions in terms of the nature and extent of their structural power. However, unionized jobs and the professions differ in the extent to which typical work situations and arrangements are defined by the policies of representative associations and schools. While professionals tend to employ technologies articulated within their occupation, most members of industrial unions tend to carry out technologies planned by management. The authority enjoyed by professionals is dervied from the normative foundations of their occupation, from the standards and principles that define their occupation's technology. Structural power is relevant only to the extent that it underscores occupational norms; the normative foundations are a more essential component of occupational authority.

Librarians would be categorized in cell 3. Along with other knowledge-based semiprofessions, librarians have a relatively well defined task domain,

Normative Foundations

	Minimal	Elaborated
Powerful	2. *Low occupational authority* Example: individuals in jobs organized by industrial unions	4. *High occupational authority* (Most if not all settings oriented toward occupation) Example: Individuals in professions, craft unions
Minimal	1. *No occupational authority* Example: individuals in jobs organized by management	3. *Variable occupational authority* (High occupational authority in settings oriented toward occupation) Example: individuals in semiprofessions, nonunionized technical specialties

Structural Foundations

Figure 2-1. Occupational Authority in Work Settings as a Function of the Interaction of the Normative and Structural Foundations of the Occupation

but, as we have seen, lack most of the structural sources of power. Technical, semiprofessional, and professional occupations, as opposed to the jobs in cells 1 and 2, possess well-defined task domains. In work settings oriented toward an occupation and the agencies that represent its interests, individual members of that occupation exercise an occupationally based authority. The distinction between cells 3 and 4 rests on the ability of professional associations and schools to enforce compliance with occupational institutions. The status honor associated with a profession as opposed to a semiprofession or nonunionized technical specialty is backed by legally defined standards of practice and a market monopoly. Occupational authority at work rests on the existence of normative foundations; powerful structural foundations ensure that those normative foundations are acknowledged in all work settings.

A reappraisal of the ability of librarians to control their own work activities rests on two distinctions regarding the location of the sources of occupational, as opposed to managerial authority, and the function of normative institutions, as opposed to structural power as sources of that authority. Occupational authority is based on the normative and structural foundations established by representative associations and schools outside the settings in which members work. Librarians derive their authority in the work setting from the standards of librarianship and library service articulated by library associations and schools. The normative standards that define how work is and ought to be organized are essential to occupational authority and control over work. Library associations have established the necessary normative foundations for the emergence of occupational authority in settings collectively oriented toward the occupation. Because the power to establish appropriate work arrangements flows from the collective endorsement within the setting of the occupation's institutions and status order, the librarian may exercise an occupationally derived authority despite their occupation's lack of the structural foundations of an established profession.

Notes

1. This distinction between status and party is relevant when consideration is given to the actions of associations and schools to establish an occupational monopoly. In separate essays Weber associates the notion of a monopoly with a status group (1946) and with a corporate group (1947, pp. 145-146, concerning the enforcement of closed social relationships). I argue here that an occupation constitutes, at the least, a corporately organized status group. However, in opposition to Weber, I further argue that occupations may be corporately organized by representative associations and schools, and that these bodies may succeed in the establishment of a status group without the occupation's also attaining a monopoly in its task domain. A monopoly is associated with a domain consensus involving employers and probably the state in addition to the occupation. Societal action taken by representative associations and schools acting in the capacity of a party is necessary for the achievement of an occupational monopoly.

2. The articulation of occupational institutions by representative associations and schools is not part of the structures of an occupation. Only the actions of those agencies that occur within the existing normative order constitute social structure as defined.

3. Cloward uses the term *learning structures* in his analysis of the distribution of deviance in society. Learning structures refer to "appropriate learning environments for the acquisition of the values and skills associated with the performance of a particular role." (1959, p. 168).

3 The Normative Foundations

This chapter describes the extent to which policy statements of library associations prescribe work arrangements for librarians and libraries without attempting to review or evaluate the degree to which the principles of library science exemplify a professional ideology or a science. Rather, the ultimate objective is to facilitate a comparison between these policy statements and actual conditions of work in library settings. As part III reports on the results of a 1974 survey of libraries and investigates the conditions associated with compliance with occupational norms, it is important that we have a clear understanding of the relevant occupational policies as they existed at that point in time.

The first part of this chapter deals with the task domain claimed for librarians by library associations. By outlining ancillary occupations, we can understand the internal organization of this domain; by comparing the educational qualifications that typify each occupational status, we can begin to appreciate the claim of expertise. A definite order of command is prescribed for the administration of libraries; even relations between librarians in the same library are conceived in hierarchical and not collegial terms.

The second part elaborates on this picture of organization within the task domain. In order to illustrate critical distinctions drawn between professional librarians and nonprofessionals, two tasks are examined in some detail: the provision of reference service and the selection of materials for acquisition. The authority structure is reflected in the allocation of tasks and in the pattern of communication that should attend performance of those tasks. These occupational role expectations reflect the implicit sense of moral responsibility and causality that underlies the standards of librarianship.

The Task Domain

In a policy statement on library education and manpower, the ALA sets out its claim for competence over a distinct task domain.

> Library service as here understood is concerned with knowledge and information in their several forms—their identification, *selection*, acquisition, preservation, organization, communication and interpretation, and *assistance in use.*
>
> To meet the goals of library service, both professional and supportive staff are needed in the libraries. Thus, the library occupation is much

broader than that segment of it which is the library profession, but *the library profession has the responsibility for defining the training and education required for the preparation of personnel who work in libraries at any level, supportive or professional* (italics added).[1]

This statement tends to be echoed in Canadian circles.[2] Librarians in the sample concurred; they saw themselves as the dominant occupation within their work settings. This perspective of dominance flavors all policy regarding the occupational structure of library service.

Occupational Status

The policies of the ALA provide a detailed, occupationally centered plan of how work is to be done. Their vocabulary labels the occupation and the other statuses with which members interact, the different types of occupations to be found within the occupation, their training and other qualifications, and the various tasks they are competent to perform. Prescriptions for occupational structures are usually some variant of the most recent ALA hierarchy of occupational statuses. In figure 3-1 each box represents a different occupational status. The gradations marked on each box indicate the possibilities for promotion within each occupation. The overlap between occupations signifies that with job experience, senior members of a subordinate occupation may receive pay and exercise responsibilities on a par with junior appointments in the next higher occupation.

This arrangement of occupations differs from earlier renditions in that an attempt has been made to identify and integrate the roles of information specialists and technicians with the more traditional positions of librarians, assistants, and clerks. Occupational titles were adjusted to acknowledge some upgrading of library service skills. "Technicians" became "technical assistants" and, to retain some recognition of the status differential, "assistants" were promoted to "associate" rank.

Although other associations, including the CLA, seem to acknowledge many of the distinctions proposed by the ALA, they continue to use more traditional occupational titles in their policy proposals and statements. The more traditional occupational titles employed in the survey questionnaire represented the distinctions recognized by most of the respondents interviewed. See table 3-1 for a comparison of titles used in the questionnaire and those used by the ALA.

Educational Qualifications

Since 1948 the ALA has sought to distinguish three types of careers in library service—those for the professional, the subprofessional, and the support staff.

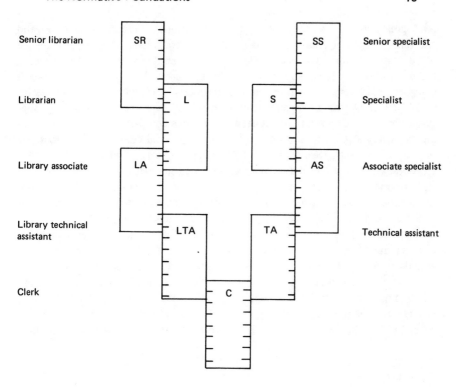

Source: "Library, Education, and Manpower," *American Libraries* 1 (1970):665.

Figure 3-1. American Library Association Hierarchy of Occupational Statuses

Table 3-1
A Comparison of Occupational Titles Used in the Questionnaire and Those Used by the American Library Association

Distinctions Recognized by Respondents in the Sample	Official ALA Categories
Professional librarian, librarian	Senior librarian, librarian
Library assistant	Library associate, and possibly associate specialist
Library technician	Library technical assistant (LTA) and technical assistant
Library clerk	Clerk
Subject area specialist	Senior specialist, specialist, and possibly associate specialist

ALA policy in 1970 stated that "until examinations are identified that are valid and reliable tests of equivalent qualifications, the academic degree (or evidence of years of academic work completed) is recommended as the single best means for determining that an applicant has the background recommended for each category ("Library Education and Manpower," *American Libraries* 1970, p. 343). Completion of a general, university-level degree program distinguishes subprofessionals from support staff. Professionals complete postgraduate training in library science in addition to having the general educational background of subprofessionals. (See table 3-2.) Although promotion would be contingent on obtaining more formal education, distinctions between senior librarians and librarians are a matter of degree of professional experience. In comparison, the distinction between technical assistants and clerks is qualitative rather than a matter of degree. However, in practice, specialized on-the-job experience can blur the distinctions between the nonprofessional statuses. With these qualifications in mind, it is obvious that in most instances additional formal education would result in promotion from one occupational status to the next.

At the present time, the only occupation challenging the traditional position of the librarian is the library technician. It is the only other occupation that receives formal training in library work. Shortly after the inception of training programs for library technicians, the library associations took action to monitor

Table 3-2
Educational Qualifications Set by the American Library Association

Career	Occupation	Formal Educational Requirements
Professional	Senior librarian, senior specialist Librarian, specialist	Beyond master's degree Master's degree[a]
Subprofessional	Library associate, associate specialist	Bachelor's degree (including work short of a master's degree)
Support	Library technical assistant, technical assistant[b]	Two years of college-level study, or Two-year program at community college, or Postsecondary training in relevant skills
	Clerk	Business school or commercial courses

Note: This table merges the careers outlined in *Descriptive List of Professional and Nonprofessional Duties in Libraries* (Chicago: ALA Board on Personnel Administration, 1948) with the 1970 ALA statement on Library Education and Manpower

[a]The master's degree was recognized as ALA policy in 1970 for the United States. As of 1973, all schools in Canada except the one at the University of Alberta accepted the MLS as the norm. (See Megrian, 1974.)

[b]"Criteria for Programs to Prepare Library Media Technical Assistants," *American Libraries* 2(1971):1059-1063.

and evaluate these courses of study.[3] The CLA issued recommendations and initiated a survey or summary of Canadian programs in 1968. In 1971 the ALA revised its 1969 policy (Ellsworth, 1973). In 1972 the CLA revised its 1968 recommendations for the training of library technicians. The following statement indicates the closeness of the relationship between the CLA and the ALA.

> The Committee on the Training of Library Technicians [CLA] is working on this revision, and in doing so intends to incorporate the basic provisions of the ALA-LED (Library Education Division) criteria statement, which we have accepted in principle, and in the drafting of which Mr. Marshall served as consultant. (Marshall and Munroe, 1971, p. 5)

(Marshall was both a consultant to the ALA on this issue and the author of the CLA recommendations issued in 1972.) The revised CLA guidelines (1972) seem to be somewhat stronger than the 1971 ALA policy. In this fourth survey of library technician programs in Canada, capsule comments were appended to the descriptive details reported on each program. These comments presented the "central conclusions about [each] program and its progress (or otherwise) towards meeting the recommended standards." The publication of this evaluation "came as a result of a felt need on the part of many librarians, including the Board of Directors of the CLA who, in reviewing the work of the Committee, strongly recommended this to the Chairman" (Marshall and Munroe, 1972, p. 3). By sponsoring a more active program at the national level, the CLA would seem to be more effective in subordinating the formal education of library technicians to criteria set by library associations.[4]

The 1970 ALA policy accepted the proposition that specialized educational qualifications unrelated to library science per se have a part to play in library service.[5] In working out the implications of this distinction, the ALA may have conveyed the impression that two distinct occupational hierarchies now exist within libraries—one based on knowledge of library science and the other on knowledge of specialized information or of information-retrieval technologies. I believe that this overstates the ALA's position. What seems to have been introduced is a distinction akin to that between line and staff within organizations. Without training in library operations, specialists and technicians are not expected to supervise or direct the activities of others. The utility of such staff increases with on-the-job training in the library. With job experience, associate specialists and technical assistants could be laterally promoted into line positions (library associate and library technical assistant, respectively). The policy states that "the suggested role of in-service training in the total program of library education clearly involves library staffs and administrators" (Asheim, 1968, p. 1103). However, by limiting the significance of in-service training to lateral promotions, the ALA has clearly claimed the right to designate intra- and interoccupational status structures, leaving only implementation to practitioners in the field. Table 3-3 compares line and staff relationships.

Table 3-3
Line and Staff Relationships between Occupational Statuses
According to the American Library Association

Line Positions	Staff Positions
Senior librarian	Senior specialist
Librarian	Specialist
Library associate[a]	Associate specialist
Library technical assistant[a]	Technical assistant

[a]LAs and LTAs may have both line and staff duties (although the line responsibilities of the LTAs are strictly limited).

Authority Structure

The task domain may be viewed as a role set (Merton, 1957) in which librarians and members of other ancillary occupations carry out their duties. The roles of the different statuses within the occupational role set are hierarchically organized. Librarians are charged with the duty to guide and supervise the others. Within the librarian's zone of competence, the others are expected to comply with the legitimate requests and directives. As demarcated along occupational lines, the entire role set constitutes the occupational task domain (Friedson, 1970, pp. 127-145).

The 1948 ALA statement, *Professional and Non-Professional Duties in Libraries*, assigns management tasks to librarians as part of their professional responsibilities. The following list of duties paraphrases the prerogatives of librarians:

1. Making plans and policy regarding library service.
2. Executing policy regarding library service.
    a. Stipulating job descriptions, and recruiting and promoting library personnel in terms of those classifications.
    b. Establishing regulations and guidelines for work carried out by library personnel.
    c. Supervising the preparation of work schedules (including detailed rules and procedures).
    d. Supervising or directing the supervision of assigned work.
    e. Developing a system of required records and statistics.
    f. Evaluating the performance and output of library personnel.
    g. Training and educating librarians and library assistants ("associates" as of 1970) on an in-service basis. In the absence of senior nonprofessionals, this would include the training and education of support staff as well.

Figures 3-2 and 3-3 indicate the pattern of interoccupational control that emerges. Librarians are the only source of formal policy, guidelines, and regulations. Librarians are also responsible for all surveillance, including close supervision and the review of records and statistics on individual and collective performance. At the discretion of librarians, senior support staff with library-related qualifications may review and supervise the work of junior support staff.

The less detailed ALA policies of twenty years later support this outline of professional authority. While experienced subprofessionals may "rely less upon specific and detailed guidance and [have] more independence of action within the regulations and guidelines established by the professional staff, . . . the work of the technical assistant is performed under direct supervision or well established guidelines within a framework of specific operating instructions and procedures."[6] Although collegiality may not be inappropriate for certain activities among professionals, a definite hierarchy of professional authority exists between librarians and nonlibrarians.[7]

An Illustration of Standards: Reference and Selection

In order to illustrate the impact of institutions of librarianship on the organization of work arrangements, a survey of settings in libraries, learning resource centers, material centers, and archives was carried out in the summer of 1974. The objective of this survey was to determine the degree of correspondence between occupational standards and organizational work arrangements. The problem of mapping roles was simplified by focusing attention on the organization of two relatively central library activities: reference service and the selection

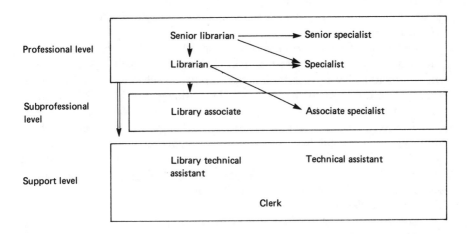

Figure 3-2. Responsibility for Setting Formal Rules and Operating Procedures

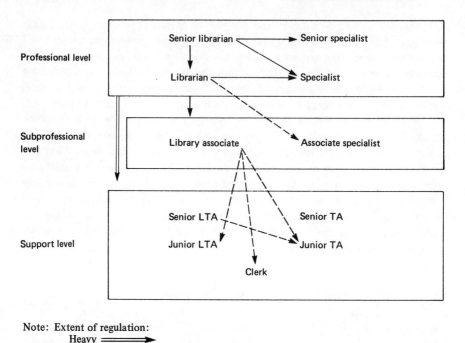

Note: Extent of regulation:
Heavy ═══════▶
Light ─────────▶
At the discretion of librarians ─ ─ ─ ─ ─▶

Figure 3-3. Responsibility for Surveillance: Close Supervision or Gathering
Information

of new materials for acquisition. (See appendix A for a description of the field
procedures used to verify the adequacy of these two activities for the purposes
of this study.)

   Providing reference service involves responding to the immediate needs of
the library's users. This service may take the form of (1) gathering and classifying information (when such information is not immediately at hand) and then
providing information to the users, or (2) providing available information, or
(3) giving directions or advice so that users can satisfy their own immediate needs.

   Selecting new materials for acquisition takes place after materials have
been suggested for purchase by users and by publishers and other sources of
materials (and before the actual processing of the acquisition order). Selecting
new materials takes the form of (1) gathering and classifying information about
suggested materials and (2) recommending which materials should be added to
the library's collection.

   Studying the organization of reference and selection activities reduced the
possibility that the survey results would merely reflect a process of diffusion.

Diffusion would probably account for many library practices followed, for example, in cataloging or circulation. Discussions with librarians suggested that, in the cases of reference and selection, applications of occupational standards and principles were more a matter of judgment than of textbook technique. Work procedures associated with these tasks are not likely to be directly copied from "textbook" guidelines.

In the survey of libraries, many questions sought task-specific information. These definitions of reference and selection were presented to the respondents in each library and discussed at the beginning of the interviews. Reference and selection would be recognized on any organizational chart. In the libraries surveyed, a considerable proportion of the time and energy of the staff were devoted to carrying out these tasks. the constituent activities of these two tasks accounted for approximately one-quarter of the professional duties of librarians as enumerated by library associations. Reference and selection tasks were central activities in terms of both work carried out in libraries and the institutions of librarianship.

Occupational Role Expectations

In the past, library associations have shown a great deal of interest in the division of labor between professional librarians and the other nonprofessional occupations. The importance of the dominant occupation is reinforced by the lines of occupational jurisdiction that define a division of labor. Central tasks are reserved exclusively for members of the dominant occupation. Reference service and the selection of materials for acquisition, the two tasks dealt with within the survey questionnaire, were explicitly considered by the ALA in 1948 and by the Library Association in 1963 and in 1974.[8] For the purposes of this survey of libraries I attempted to define these two activities in terms of the conceptions and behaviors found in the work settings included in the sample. As defined, the selection of material ranked as the only professional activity. Reference service turned out to be a composite of three activities: preparing bibliographies, providing information, and giving directions. The first subtask was regarded as highly professional in nature, the second as primarily professional, and the third as a task that could appropriately be performed by any experienced or knowledgeable member of a library's staff.[9] There was consensus on these judgments across associations, and the large number of articles and books on the general topic of the division of labor between professionals and nonprofessionals testifies to the considerable interest in the question.[10]

Recently, the ALA has shown signs of shifting its basic stance from a concern about professionals doing nonprofessional tasks to a concern about nonprofessionals performing professional tasks. Before, carrying out nonprofessional tasks was viewed as a threat to the prestige and status of librarians. Now it seems that the threat posed by the new information technologies to the occupation's jurisdiction and dominance is considered to be of greater importance. When introducing proposals for new policies ("Education and Manpower for Librarianship," 1968, p. 1097), the ALA alluded to the specific duties of librarians only once. "Any basic library procedure—cataloguing, classification, *reference work, book selection,* work with the library's publics—requires the application of the librarian's skill to the material of the subject" (italics added). In an article following up the 1970 statement of policy, the sin of actually performing nonprofessional tasks was qualified. "There is a difference between a professional's being willing to do nonprofessional tasks if necessary and having them written in as part of his job description" (Asheim, 1971, p. 599). The ALA, in "Library Education and Manpower" (1970), did not attempt to enumerate the professional duties of librarians in any detail.

In comparison to librarians, the distinction between professional and nonprofessional duties was drawn explicitly and in detail for library technical assistants. "Criteria for Programs to Prepare Library/Media Technical Assistants" (1971), issued by the same office that prepared the 1970 policy on librarianship, enumerated the specific tasks that library and media technical assistants (LMTAs) ought and ought not do. "Establishment of policies, *materials selection, complex information and guidance services*" (p. 1060, italics added) constituted one of four sets of tasks explicitly excluded from the work of the LMTA (Library/Media Technical Assistants). The following components of reference work were among the six sets of tasks that LMTAs could appropriately perform: "Circulation work such as . . . explaining lending rules. . . . Information services work such as: (1) Answering directional or factual questions. . . . (2) Locating bibliographical information for which complex searching is not required. (3) Acquisitions work such as . . . ordering materials (*exclusive of selection*)." (p. 1061, italics added). At this time, it was again made clear that LMTAs could not select materials. The attention once devoted to the activities of librarians is now focused on the activities performed by potentially competing occupations.

Some of the ALA policies on the division of labor have been endorsed by the CLA. The CLA came into existence in 1947, one year before the ALA published its document on this subject. The CLA immediately subscribed to the ALA's system of accreditation. The CLA did not issue any statement on professional and nonprofessional duties. The issue of professional duties may not have been regarded as an essential piece of business. However, the CLA is acting in accord with the ALA on more recent policies regarding library technicians. The Committee on the Training of Library Technicians accepted in principle the basic provisions of the 1971 ALA policy and intended to incorporate them into CLA policy proposals. Its draft on the duties of library technicians, while briefer than the ALA statement on LMTAs, essentially corresponds to standards set south of the border. Library technicians cannot participate in the selection of materials and are restricted to providing "quick reference and directional information" (Marshall and Munroe, 1972, p. 5).

Given that policies of the various associations are either dated, piecemeal, or nonspecific. tables 3-4 and 3-5 only approximate the occupational standards with respect to allocation of reference and selection tasks. Using the occupational titles listed in the survey questionnaire, the division of labor shown in table 3-5 is prescribed by library association standards. Most librarians would be expected to be available to handle more complex reference work and may be asked to provide all types of reference services. Some but not necessarily all librarians would be expected to select material for acquisition. All nonprofessionals—library assistants, library technicians, and library clerks—would be excluded from selection activities. If directed to do so by a librarian, a nonprofessional could appropriately provide simple reference service, passing on more complex work to a librarian.

An Occupational Technology and the Pattern of Communication

The system of work as idealized by occupational institutions has a causal and moral texture. Interpreted in the context of those institutions, particular events

Table 3-4
Standards Governing Participation in Selection and Reference Activities

Level	Occupations	Other Contributors
Selection		

Professionals only	Librarians[a]	Library staff
		  Subject area specialists
		Library clientele
		  Faculty (educational libraries)
		  Executives, researchers, technicians
		  (special libraries)

Reference		*Duties*
Professional	Librarians and subject area specialist (at the discretion of librarians)	Providing bibliographies Providing information
Nonprofessional[b]	Any trained or experienced member of staff	Providing directions

[a]In addition to nominating materials on their own, librarians are expected to seek suggestions from professional-level clients and specialists. However, final decisions regarding materials to be acquired rest solely with librarians.

[b]It is appropriate for nonprofessionals to field initial requests for assistance if they refer the more complex requests to librarians.

Table 3-5
Prescribed Role Expectations for Selection and Reference Activities, by Occupation

Occupational Titles	Reference	Selection
Professional librarians	Yes[a]	Yes[a]
Subject area specialists	Vague	Vague
Library assistants	Qualified yes	No
Library technicians	Qualified yes	No
Library clerks	Qualified yes	No

[a]Librarians may legitimately do only reference or only selection.

and work arrangements take on a distinct meaning. Procedures involving the sequential or joint performance of a set of tasks convey a sense of causality. The manner in which one task is carried out—its timing, location, or style of performance—is typically claimed to have predictable consequences for the performance of joint or subsequent tasks, whether or not those consequences have been verified. In a similar vein, personal qualifications, especially those relating to prior training or job experience, are thought to have a direct bearing on ability to adequately perform occupational tasks. Contingencies of a causal nature link the actions of subordinates and clients or employers, on the one hand, with the work performed by members of the occupation, on the other. The task domain is regarded as a system of action with a distinct causal texture.

Occupational standards and principles also typically convey a sense of moral or ontological necessity over and above any notions of causality or typicality that may exist. Certain problems *must* be alleviated; prescribed courses of action *must* be followed when attending to such duties. Specific tasks *must* be performed only by members of the senior occupation. Members of that occupation *must* supervise some types of work done by those in auxiliary positions. The sense of responsibility, duty, and leadership implicit in the claim of competence contributes to the sense of purpose associated with each task, procedure, and role in the occupational work setting.

> Instrumental action is rooted on the one hand in desired outcomes and on the other hand in beliefs about cause/effect relationships. To the extent that the activities dictated by man's beliefs are judged to produce desired outcomes, we can speak of technology, or technical rationality. (Thompson, 1967, p. 14)

To the extent that occupational work practices are dictated by cause-effect beliefs and are judged to produce desired outcomes, we can speak of an *occupational technology*.[11]

The causal and moral texture implicit in policy statements of library associations suggests a pattern of communication that is consistent with the authority structure and the division of labor. The task requirements spelled out in the ALA and Library Association (LA, United Kingdom) statements on professional and nonprofessional activities might be consistent with the causal ordering shown in table 3-6.

The linear character of this causal sequence (see figure 3-4) may be a product of the desire of librarians to be professionals. "Library Education and Manpower" (1970, p. 341) reserves to librarians the right to define the needs of library users: "In defining services to users, the professional person recognizes potential users as well as current ones, and designs services which will reach all who could benefit from them." The processes as schematically illustrated require that the librarian anticipate the needs of users. In effect, the needs of an individual patron for reference service are defined in terms of policy governing library services, information available in the existing library collection, and the skills of the mediating library staff. In turn, the content of the library's collection is defined by policy on library service and by librarians

Table 3-6
Factors Affecting the Selection of Materials and the Provision of Reference Services

Activity	Determining Factors
Selection	
Policy	Decisions on which groups should be served, and the extent and kind of service to be provided
Knowledge	General knowledge about subject areas, and the availability of new materials (gained through reading and use of bibliographical aids)
Statistics	Rates of withdrawal, material on reserve lists, interlibrary loan requests, formal surveys of users; informal contacts initiated with readers

Consultation	Library users with specialized knowledge
	   Faculty, in education libraries;
	   Executive, research workers and technicians, in special libraries;
	   Professional staff in contact with readers, in public libraries.

Reference	
Policy	Same as for selection
Knowledge	Location of available sources of information in the library[a]
Skill	Reference techniques

[a]By directing library users to certain information, statistics on withdrawals, reserve lists, and interlibrary loan requests may be affected. Reference activity might affect the mass reading habits of the libraries and thereby indirectly have an effect on the statistics compiled to guide the selection.

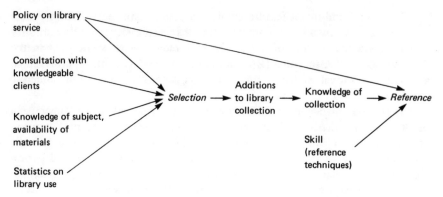

Figure 3-4. The Causal Sequence of Selection and Reference Activities

who identify the availability of materials, who develop and interpret statistics on library use, and who solicit and screen suggestions made by others. The ALA's Library Bill of Rights (1939, 1948, 1967) claims for librarians all rights of determination of library holdings and service, explicitly denying such rights to clients and the public at large.

These policies encourage librarians who select materials to develop their own set of indicators of "needed" materials, indicators subject to their own control and initiative. They are not encouraged to react to current or immediate requests for reference assistance when making their selections. In the 1948 ALA and 1963 and 1974 LA documents, there was no hint that bibliographies or information produced in the course of providing reference would be an input into the selection process. Of course the use of reference work generated for clients as a guide for selection is conceivable, and may actually occur in many libraries. The point is that the otherwise specific and detailed prescriptions regarding selection *omit* any allusion to this obvious possibility. Librarians are expected to take the initiative in obtaining information and in supervising the work of other occupational statuses. In terms of the pattern of communication, these policies require that those who select materials for acquisition (the librarian) initiate contacts with those who provide reference service.

Conclusions

The standards of librarianship and library service articulated by central library associations define the librarian's task domain. The occupations identified within the task domain are ordered into a relatively clear authority hierarchy. Each occupation is differentiated from the others in terms of requisite educational qualifications. Librarians are distinguished from nonlibrarians by their advanced and specialized formal education. While librarians may perform a variety of tasks, nonlibrarians are explicitly excluded from more professional activities such as the selection of materials for acquisition. In keeping with their position of authority, librarians are expected to take the initiative in supervising and guiding nonlibrarians. As prescribed by central library associations, the normative foundations of the librarian occupation provide a relatively clear and elaborate blueprint for work arrangements in library work settings.

Notes

1. "Library, Education, and Manpower," *American Libraries* 1(1970): 341. Reprinted with permission. The portions of the quotation that were italicized highlighted aspects of the statement of particular relevance to this study—the selection of materials for acquisition and the provision of reference service ("assistance in use").

Since 1974, the ALA has revised its goals.

The goal of the American Library Association is the promotion of libraries and librarianship to assure the delivery of user-oriented library and information* services to all. (*Information as used here includes ideas, the product of man's creative endeavors, facts, and data.) ["Epilogue to a Midwinter's Tale," *American Libraries* 6(1975):231. See also "ALA Goals and Objectives, Revised draft," *American Libraries* 6(1975):39-41]

This statement is accompanied by a planning chart that distinguishes between objectives and courses of action. This document denotes a shift toward political action—lobbying government, mobilizing public relations, stimulating research—to ensure control over library services.

2. For example, for an explicit statement, see R.C. Ellsworth (1973, p. 122): see the Canadian Association of College and University Libraries, *Position Classification and Principles of Academic Status in Canadian University Libraries* (Ottawa: Canadian Library Association, 1969), for implicit agreement.

3. Ellsworth (1973), noting that Library Technician (LT) programs were offered primarily by junior and community colleges, suggested that the emergence of Library Technician programs coincided with the expansion in the numbers of these colleges.

4. The reaction from Fanshawe College (1973) to an unfavorable review would seem to indicate that the evaluation must exert some leverage. The actions of the associations seem to indicate that, at least in Canada, library technicians will be drawn into the labor force in a way that conforms to the wishes

of librarians. In 1970 the CLA sponsored a workshop on the role of the library technicians (*The Library Technician at Work: Theory and Practice*, Proceedings of a Workshop held at Lakehead University, Thunder Bay, Ontario, 8-9 May 1970). A national association, proposed at this workshop, has failed to materialize. Provincial associations, however, have been formed. In 1975 the Alberta Association of Library Technicians (1974) was in the process of seeking affiliation with the library Association of Alberta.

5. Asheim, L. Education and Manpower for Librarianship," *American Library Association Bulletin* 1968, p. 1098.

6. Ibid., 1098, 1099. For congruent statements, see "Library Education and Manpower," *American Libraries* 1(1970):342, and "Criteria for Programs to Prepare Library/Media Technical Assistants," *American Libraries* 2 (1971):1060.

7. This image of professional authority is articulated also by the United Kingdom's Library Association and by the Canadian Association of College and University Libraries, one of the more outspoken divisions of the CLA. *Professional and Non-Professional Duties in Libraries* (1963, 1974 revision). Also see *Position Classification and Principles of Academic Status in Canadian University Libraries* (1969).

8. *A Descriptive List of Professional and Non-Professional Duties in Libraries* (Chicago, Illinois: American Library Association, 1948). See also *Professional and Non-Professional Duties in Libraries* (1963, 1974).

9. A job-task index ranked selection and reference activities in exactly the same order. The correlation between the index that included these activities and the professional status of respondents in medical libraries in the United States was r = 0.706 (Rothenberg et al. 1971).

10. Although the CLA has remained silent on this question, the fact that the Library Association (LA, United Kingdom) has recently reaffirmed its earlier policy based on the 1948 ALA document suggests a continuing consensus. This, plus the fact that the CLA has endorsed some ALA professional standards and taken issue with none, implies that ALA and LA policies on the professional-nonprofessional division of labor would be the model in Canada. See Bishop (1973) and Christianson (1973, pp. 23-37, 41-45) for a review of some of this literature.

11. According to this reasoning, even a rudimentary system of understandings, as for example that provided by maxims and proverbs in some cultures, could provide the basis of a technology. According to Galbraith (1971, p. 12), "technology means the systematic application of scientific or other organized knowledge to practical tasks." Technology is lodged neither in the nature of things per se nor in the scientific organization of knowledge. A system of occupational rules of conduct as well as managerial planning constitute organized bodies of knowledge, both of which stipulate desired outcomes and cause-effect beliefs. Either one may provide the basis for a technology.

4

Occupational Orientations: Variation from One Library to Another

Library associations define a task domain for librarians, but they have not established market and legal structures that enforce standards of librarianship. Librarians, along with members of other technical and semiprofessional occupations, are in no position to insist that their clients, employers, organizational superiors and subordinates, or the public at large comply with occupational norms. Nevertheless, there may be occasions in which others accede to occupational authority. It seems plausible that, in most instances, even management would assent to occupational work practices, even though the literature on bureaucratic-professional or line-staff relations highlights the potential for conflict. Management may endorse the task domain as organized by an occupation rather than design and implement an alternative of its own. Even if the occupation's technology is not esoteric and the occupation itself does not enjoy a preponderance of power, existing work arrangements frequently prevail over new forms of organization. The start-up costs of new work arrangements are sunken costs for established arrangements. The existence of standardized occupational practices and procedures permits the rapid organization of new work settings, making it easier to combine and integrate new staff. Institutionally standardized arrangements facilitate the organization and coordination of work in such situations. New practices, unique to a single organization, are usually poorly integrated with the wider systems of social organization—especially the educational systems and labor markets that are sources of personnel. Whether considered in terms of their efficiency or legitimacy, occupational practices are recognized and practical modes of organizing.[1]

Management incorporates these preexisting structures into their organization by developing job descriptions for organizational positions that are congruent with performance capabilities of occupational members; hiring personnel qualified to hold positions in the occupational role set; and delegating discretion and authority to members of the dominant occupation in the role set. This is not to suggest that the authority wielded by the members of that occupation is derived from management. The structure of the role set reflects the source of order provided by the external social and economic foundations of the dominant occupation. While practitioners exercising occupational authority would be supported within the organization as if they were carrying out work authorized by their managerial supervisors, the forms of their work arrangements are modeled on occupational institutions. The supposed delegation of discretion and authority by the management actually constitutes a voluntary endorsement of the occupational task domain within the organization's work setting. Compliance with occupational norms need not require either the threat or the exercise of structural power by the occupation on behalf of its members.

To sum up, it is clear that the librarian occupation cannot enforce compliance with occupational standards in the organizations that employ librarians. However, there are reasons to believe that nonlibrarians including managers may find it advantageous to endorse occupational standards of work on a voluntary basis. We may therefore, expect standards of librarianship to be acknowledged in some library work settings but not others and, as a consequence, that work arrangements may conform to standards of librarianship in some settings but not in others.

Collective Occupational Orientations

How can we identify those libraries that subscribe to occupational norms and differentiate them from those that do not? The procedure used to answer this question involves measuring the "collective occupational orientations" of all those who worked together in a library. Essentially, library clerks and library assistants as well as librarians were asked about the general awareness, interest, and relevance of the occupation in their work group. (In contrast to many studies of professionalism, this study did not measure the personal values, beliefs, and commitment of librarians.) Occupational authority is thought to rest essentially on the conjunction of (1) occupational institutions articulated outside the setting by representative associations and schools and (2) a collective orientation within the setting toward those institutions and representative agencies. According to the survey, the extent of collective orientation toward the occupation varied widely, with occupational orientations pervasive in some library work settings (figure 4-1a) and all but nonexistent in others (figure 4-1b). A collective occupational orientation links the setting with the normative foundations of the occupation and establishes the relevance of occupational institutions to work arrangements in the library.

"Orientation" for a collectivity such as a work setting is akin to "identification" for an individual. To the extent that members of a library work setting identify the collective interests and affairs of their setting with the interests and affairs of the occupation, that setting is said to be collectively oriented toward the occupation. Where such a collective occupational orientation exists, attention in the setting is directed toward the agencies that represent the interests of the occupation. The library staff expresses a collective interest in the affairs of the occupation as a whole and possesses some collective familiarity with the structure of the occupation. The principles and standards articulated by those representative agencies are regarded as relevant and applicable to conduct within the setting.

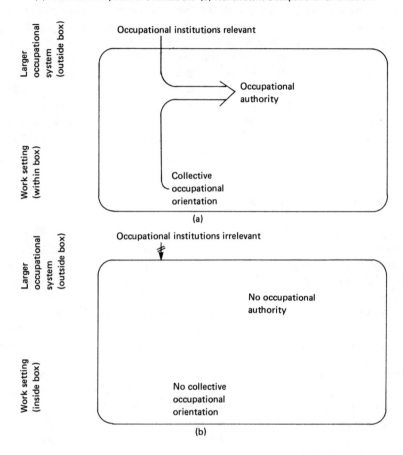

(a) Pervasive Occupational Orientation. (b) Nonexistent Occupational Orientation.

Figure 4-1. Occupational Authority within Work Settings as a Product of
Normative Processes within and outside the Work Setting.

Data on orientation were obtained from as many respondents in the setting
as it was feasible to interview. An attempt was made to include in the interview
at least one representative of each occupational status. From two to four informants were interviewed in each setting. Because of the small number of respondents, care was taken in the wording of the question and in the aggregation of
the collective score to emphasize shared understandings.

Three facets of occupational orientation were measured: (1) the extent of
reported collective interest in professional librarians as an occupation, (2) the
extent to which the interests and values of the occupation were considered to

coincide with those in the library work setting, and (3) the extent to which staff members were aware of the associations that represent the occupation. The first two indicators represent orientation toward the occupation as a status group; the last focuses on orientation toward the corporate structure of the occupation.

The collective nature of orientation was assessed in two different ways. One procedure was simply to ask respondents "to report the prevailing orientations held by the people in this library [library department]." The informants directly characterized the properties of their work setting. A second procedure first determined personal orientations and then combined the answers of the respondents to obtain a composite score that represented both the extent and the intensity of orientations in the setting.

Orientation toward Librarians as a Status Group

The first procedure was used to measure interests in professional librarians as an occupational group and the extent to which the values and interests characteristic of their setting were felt to coincide with those of the occupation. When measuring orientations toward librarians as a status group, each respondent was asked to report on readily verbalized norms, norms that were commonly acknowledged by the others in the setting. According to Zelditch (1962), it is reasonable to interview only a few informants to obtain this type of information. The items reported in table 4-1 avoid the problem of combining individual scores to yield a collective score by asking the respondents to report directly on the orientations of themselves and others in their setting.

The results from an analysis of variance suggest that the respondents were able to comply with this instruction. Respondents working in the same library setting tended to report similar answers to these items. (The differences between settings were much greater than the differences within settings.) Respondents in the same occupation in different settings did not tend to report similar interests or coincidences of interests and values. For example, librarians as a group might have tended to report higher levels of identification than clerks, no matter which setting they were in. *This did not occur.*

The answers of different respondents in the library setting were aggregated by calculating the percentage reporting a high level of collective occupational orientations in the setting—a procedure that produces a high score only if there is consensus among the informants. The level of orientation represented by the fraction of respondents reporting a relatively high level of interest or coincidence of interests and values. In one-third of the settings most respondents reported that the values and interests of the library setting coincided to a great extent with those of professional librarians (table 4-1). In these cases, according to the judgment of the respondents, their work was oriented toward the principles and standards of that occupation. In only four settings were the interests

Table 4-1
Orientation toward Professional Librarians as a Status Group

Score		Percentage of respondents in library reporting "To a great extent" or "Almost completely"	Coincidence of Values and Interests Item[a]: To what extent would you say that the values or interests of this library coincide with the values and interests of professional librarians?	
			Frequency	Percentage
3	High	71-100	11	34.4
2		41-70	12	37.5
1		1-40	5	15.6
0	Low	0	4	12.5
		Totals	32	100.0

Score		Percentage of respondents in library reporting "Very interested" or "Extremely interested"	Interest in Professional Librarians Item[a]: How interested in *this library* in how well professional librarians as a whole are getting along in the libraries of this province or country?	
			Frequency	Percentage
3	High	71-100	3	9.4
2		41-70	13	40.6
1		1-40	6	18.7
0	Low	0	10	31.3
		Totals	32	100.0

[a]The items were presented as part of the questionnaire. The questions were read aloud by the interviewer and the respondents independently recorded their own answers. These two items were adapted from questions used by Converse and Campbell (1960, p. 301) to measure personal identification with a status group to which the individual nominally belonged. It was assumed that orientation for a library setting (a collectivity) is analogous to identification for an individual.

and values of professional librarians rejected as a rationale for library operations. The professed level of interest in the fate of librarians was somewhat lower than the reported level of correspondence between organizational and occupational values and interests. In about one-third of the settings no one reported being "very interested" in how well librarians were getting along. These indicators revealed differences between settings in their orientation toward professional librarians (their connection with the occupation).

Awareness of Library Associations

Orientation toward representative associations was calculated from data on the personal awareness of individual respondents of the existence of library associations. Each respondent was presented with a list of forty-six associations and asked to put a check beside those associations they were aware of. They were instructed verbally that they need only be aware of the existence of an association, nothing more, in order to give it a check.

The list of associations was created during discussions with librarians prior to the design of the survey instrument. As a result of initial analysis of the data, consideration was restricted to twelve of the forty-six associations. Greater awareness was reported for these twelve associations than for the others. Librarians as a whole tended to "keep track of some of their issues and policies," while nonlibrarians expressed some awareness of their existence.

Data on the twelve most recognized associations are reported in table 4-2.[2] Although librarians as a whole were about as aware of one type of association as another, this was not the case for nonlibrarians. For assistants and clerks every central association was at least as well known as the most recognized specialist association. The size and inclusiveness of the geographical domains of central associations correspond to the degree to which librarians and clerks (but not assistants) were aware of them. In general, the more inclusive associations—central as opposed to specialist, national associations as opposed to local associations—tended to be more widely recognized.

Librarians have a decided edge over nonlibrarians in the extent of their awareness of all associations except the Alberta Association of Library Technicians (AALT). Such a difference does not distinguish library assistants from clerks. The most striking finding was that no association was known to all respondents. Even among those labeled professional librarians, no association was universally known. From another perspective, these data indicate that awareness was not restricted to librarians. Some members of each occupation were aware of each association.

The aggregation procedure for producing collective scores placed a premium on awareness extending across different levels of authority in a setting. Although the awareness of the person in charge is of greater importance, its salience in the work setting is muted if subordinates are oblivious to references that might be made regarding these associations and their policies. Where both subordinates and superiors recognize the existence of the associations, collective awareness of the occupational structures of librarians is regarded as high, and knowledge of these associations is likely to be considered relevant to work in the setting. Where the evidence indicated that personal awareness did not span different levels of authority, collective awareness was deemed low at best. The coding rules in table 4-3 specify the distribution of awareness associated with each successive level of collective orientation.

The aggregated score measured the distribution of personal awareness in the setting. A high score can be produced only when personal awareness is shared by nonlibrarians as well as librarians. Table 4–4 presents data on the collective awareness of each association. Again, we find that the more inclusive

Table 4-2
Individual Awareness of Library Associations
(*percent*)

	Aware of Existence			
Library Associations	Librarians (N=46)	Assistants (N=18)	Clerks (N=15)	Total[a] (N=92)
Specialist				
Canadian Association of College and University Libraries (CLA)	93.5	38.9	26.7	68.5
Canadian Association of Special Libraries and Information Services (CLA)	93.5	33.3	13.3	66.3
Association of College and Research Libraries (ALA)	91.3	22.2	26.7	63.0
Special Library Association	91.3	33.3	20.0	63.0
Canadian Library Trustees Association (CLA)	78.3	5.6	20.0	51.1
Pacific North-West Library Association	69.6	16.7	6.7	42.4
Central				
American Library Association	97.8	66.7	86.7	90.2
Canadian Library Association	97.8	88.9	80.0	90.2
Library Association of Alberta	97.8	66.7	80.0	87.0
Edmonton Library Association	87.0	50.0	60.0	76.1
Association of Alberta Library Technicians	60.9	61.1	66.7	65.2
Foothills Library Association	73.9	38.9	26.7	57.6

[a] Includes four subject area specialists and nine library technicians in addition to the seventy-nine professional librarians, library assistants, and library clerks.

associations tended to be more widely recognized. The rank order of the associations listed under each type reflects the relative number of library settings collectively aware of each association. This rank order is almost identical to that for individual awareness.[3] For the central associations the hierarchy of awareness is almost perfectly correlated with the size of their geographical domains. An inspection of the data reveals a second important fact. For eleven of the twelve associations, collective awareness ranged from one extreme to the other on the scale. Combining the scores of individuals to produce an indicator of collective awareness did not appreciably reduce the range or variance. Most of the differences in awareness occur between respondents in different libraries, not between respondents in the same library setting. That is, individuals with

Table 4-3

Coding Rules for the Collective Awareness of Specialist and Central Library Associations

Distribution of Awareness between Superior and Subordinates			
Superior (Person in Charge)		Subordinates	Score
No	and	50 percent or less	0
No	and	51 percent or more	1
Yes	and	None	
Yes	and	1-50 percent	2
Yes	and	51 percent or more	3

Note: For the collective awareness of six associations, the scores for each association were summed, yielding a scale ranging from 0 (6 × 0) to 18 (6 × 3).

the same level of personal awareness are likely to be found working together in the same library. These results suggest that personal awareness is closely linked to the level of collective awareness in the work setting. This finding increases our confidence that the combined score represents the collective orientation of the setting, even though only a few respondents were interviewed in each case.

Two indexes of collective awareness, one for each type of association, were created by adding together the scores for each association; the results are reported in table 4-5. A finding consistent with the results on the previous tables is that central associations tend to be better known than specialist associations. The extreme range in scores—from eighteen to zero for specialist associations and from eighteen to three for central associations—indicates that summing the scores emphasizes the differences in collective awareness from one setting to another. High collective awareness of one association tends to be associated with a collective awareness of the others. On the other hand, scores ranging from zero to four indicate that some library settings are virtually unaware of all the associations. Just as individuals working in the same setting tend to display similar levels of personal awareness, the level of collective awareness of one association tends to be similar to the level of collective awareness of the others. These indexes probably measure a diffuse awareness of a system of library associations rather than a more narrowly focused interest in individual associations as discrete and independent entities.

All four indicators of orientation toward librarians and library associations are positively correlated. Although specialist associations were not as widely recognized as central associations, collective awareness of one type of association is closely related to collective awareness of the other. This finding reinforces the interpretation that these indicators tap a diffuse awareness of a system of library associations. While library staff tended to report a higher coincidence of values and interest in the occupation where awareness of library associations

Table 4-4
Collective Awareness of Library Associations
(*percent*)

	Collective Awareness			
Library Associations	*Nil (0)*	*Low (1)*	*Moderate (2)*	*High (3)*
Central				
American Library Association	– (0)	9.4 (3)	15.6 (5)	75.0 (24)
Canadian Library Association	3.1 (1)	3.1 (1)	15.6 (5)	78.0 (25)
Library Association of Alberta	3.1 (1)	15.6 (5)	12.5 (4)	68.8 (22)
Edmonton Library Association	6.3 (2)	21.9 (7)	25.0 (8)	46.9 (15)
Association of Alberta Library Technicians	25.0 (8)	25.0 (8)	15.6 (5)	34.4 (11)
Foothills Library Association	28.1 (9)	21.9 (7)	25.0 (8)	25.0 (8)
Specialist				
Canadian Association of College and University Libraries (CLA)	12.5 (4)	18.8 (6)	34.4 (11)	34.4 (11)
Canadian Association of Special Libraries and Information Services (CLA)	6.3 (2)	21.9 (7)	40.6 (13)	31.3 (10)
Special Library Association	6.3 (2)	31.3 (10)	37.5 (12)	25.0 (8)
Association of College and Research Libraries (ALA)	9.4 (3)	28.1 (9)	37.5 (12)	25.0 (8)
Canadian Library Trustees Association	25.0 (8)	28.1 (9)	34.4 (11)	12.5 (4)
Pacific North-West Library Association	28.1 (11)	40.6 (13)	21.9 (7)	9.4 (3)

Note: Frequencies are given in parentheses.

was high (and vice versa), the correlation was not perfect. In some settings in which the respondents were highly aware of library associations, respondents felt that their organizational goals differed from the standards of librarianship articulated by these associations.

Conclusions

There were considerable differences between the library work settings sampled. The variance was most pronounced for the measures of collective awareness of library associations. In a few settings nonlibrarians as well as librarians were

Table 4-5
Indexes of Collective Awareness of Library Associations

	Six Central Associations		Six Specialist Associations	
Awareness	*Frequency*	*Percent*	*Frequency*	*Percent*
17-18 High	6	18.7	2	6.3
15-16	7	21.9	2	6.3
13-14	6	18.7	6	18.7
11-12	6	18.7	5	15.6
9-10	3	9.4	6	18.7
7-8	2	6.3	3	9.4
5-6	0	–	4	12.5
3-4	2	6.3	1	3.1
1-2	0	–	2	6.3
0 Low	0	–	1	3.1
Total	32	100.0	32	100.0

aware of all the central and specialist library associations included in the indexes. In other settings, by contrast, not even the person in charge was aware of more than one or two of these associations. If, as hypothesized, a collective occupational orientation establishes the relevance of occupational institutions to organizational work arrangements, only some library settings are predicted to accord librarians professional status or to have work arrangements that conform to occupational norms.

Notes

1. See Stinchcombe (1965) on the liability of newness, especially on the problems associated with learning new roles, coordinating new roles, and recruiting strangers. See Meyer and Rowan (1977) on the issue of legitimation of organizational positions and arrangements.

2. This statement must be qualified. Slightly more respondents were aware of the Canadian Association of Public Libraries (CAPL) than were aware of the AALT (65.2 percent as opposed to 60.9 percent, respectively). The AALT was included in this index because jurisdictional conflicts were emerging between librarians and library technicians. As a central issue for the occupation, recognition of the AALT probably represented some appreciation of the structure of the occupation of professional librarians. The AALT was thus included even though it did not represent librarians and was in the process of becoming incorporated at the time.

3. The Special Libraries Associations and the Association of College and Research Libraries are practically tied on both tables, with the former ranked ahead of the latter on collective awareness and vice versa on individual awareness. The ranks of the other ten associations do not vary from one table to the other.

5 Control over Work in Occupationally Oriented Libraries

The librarian occupation is corporately organized. While several associations claim to represent the interests of librarians, their prescriptions for the occupation are not in conflict. For example, the CLA has taken care to integrate its policies on library technicians with those of the ALA. On other matters, such as the accreditation of schools of library science, the CLA has endorsed, explicitly or implicitly, the policies of the ALA. While the occupation lacks the structural foundations of a profession, the associations representing its interests, particularly the ALA, have articulated standards of librarianship. These standards define the occupation's task domain. Within that domain a clear division of labor and hierarchy of authority is demarcated. In particular, these occupational institutions prescribe appropriate conduct and states of affairs vis-á-vis the provision of reference service and the selection of materials for acquisition.

Library associations appear to be able to focus the image of the occupation even though the interests of librarians are represented by a multitude of loosely organized associations. In terms of formal structure, the corporate organization of the occupation is polycentric. Yet the results of the survey suggest that the normative foundations of the occupation are relatively coherent. There are few if any inconsistencies between the policies advocated by different library associations. Library associations have moved to minimize differences that do appear. This appearance of accord is reflected in the normative orientations toward these associations. Individuals had a diffuse awareness of library associations. For example, awareness of the ALA or CLA was indicative of a general awareness of a variety of other prominent associations. For associations that claimed to represent a geographical area, the size of their domain was a perfect predictor of the level of awareness of the association for both librarians and nonlibrarians. The pattern of awareness of library associations follows lines of jurisdiction defined by the associations and does not reveal any sense of ideological division.

As of 1974, the date of the library survey, the library associations' claim to represent the interests of librarians and librarianship had not been seriously challenged by labor unions. However, the trend toward unionization of library workers may disrupt the normative foundations of the librarian occupation. The ideological gap between library associations and labor unions is manifested in a union's emphasis on negotiating salaries and benefits, assisting member's grievances, and lobbying for laws regulating conditions of work (Biblartz et al., 1975). The unionization of nonlibrarians to the exclusion of librarians would not only restrict the librarian's freedom to organize library operations but would also tend to reorient nonlibrarians away from the library occupation, possibly reducing collective occupational orientations and attenuating the occupational authority of the librarian in the work setting. The unionization of the librarians may pose even greater problems for the occupation. Labor relations boards have had serious reservations about letting librarians join labor unions because librarians carry out many managerial responsibilities and duties (Schroeder, 1975). To the extent that unionization is achieved by minimizing or relinquishing the librarian's "rights" to organize library operations and supervise the work of others, unionization would violate the standards of librarianship and library service advocated by library associations. The legitimacy of the occupational dominance order promoted by library associations would be drawn into question. If unionization is accompanied by a redefinition of the status of the librarian from "manager of library operations" to "library employee", unionization will attack the institutional source of authority for all librarians, whether or not their particular library was undergoing unionization. An investigation of the actual policies of labor unions that are actively organizing librarians would be required in order to determine the impact of this movement on the status of the librarian in the work setting.

The normative foundations of the librarian occupation constitute an institutional context that may or may not be acknowledged in the library work settings included in the survey. The results of the survey indicate that the presence of librarians and the level of collective occupational orientations varies considerably from one setting to another. If these data reflect the extent to which occupational standards are voluntarily endorsed, we would expect occupational control over work to be greatest in libraries where awareness of library associations was high and where the interests and values of the staff were aligned with the occupation.

**Part II
The Impact of Standards of
Librarianship in Library
Work Settings**

Standardized arrangements within libraries can be at least partially accounted for in terms of occupational control over work. Library associations and schools of library science have constructed a set of institutional standards and principles that define how library service should be organized in libraries. Berger and Luckman have noted that "institutions . . . control human conduct by setting up predefined patterns of conduct, which channel it in one direction as against the many other directions that would theoretically be possible. . . . This controlling character is inherent in institutionalization as such, prior to or apart from any mechanisms of sanctions specifically set up to support an institution" (1966, p. 55). It is important not to gloss over the last point. The controlling character of the policies of library associations exists prior to or apart from any market or legal structures that might enforce those policies. By defining the task domain of the occupation, library associations and schools have created the potential for regulating conduct within the libraries that employ librarians.

Work arrangements legitimized as applications of occupational institutions tend to be formalized. "Formalization is the degree to which the norms of a social system are explicit." (Price, 1972, p. 107.) The language used by library associations and schools categorizes and labels the types of personnel, their tasks, and typical patterns of work arrangements. This language enables understandings on the job to be expressed explicitly—either verbally or in written form.[1]

Formal role expectations are established by matching the activities in a setting with abstract institutional beliefs about situations "like this one." The situation is interpreted *as if* it were an embodiment of an institutional order—in the manner of a simile, the institutional knowledge base "explains" the situation at hand. The institutional order defines the classes of activities that may be expected to occur and the types of individuals who may be expected to be present and participate in the setting. By considering the context of an action or event defined in this manner, one is able to ascertain the purposes as well as the motives of those involved. Formal rules and procedures are judged more by their logical consistency and their moral or causal implications within the framework of occupational institutions than by their suitability for the individual within the work setting.[2]

Role expectations that can be justified, rationalized, or explained in terms of well-established practices, customs, or laws gain a dimension of meaning that transcends interpersonal experience in the setting. In an important sense, institutionalized role expectations have an existence that is independent of their implementation in any local work setting. The techniques they embody are articulated by library associations and schools of library science outside the work setting. Instead of being founded on shared interpersonal experiences within the library, occupational practices are based upon standards and principles of an abstract and general nature. As a consequence, occupational norms have the impersonal and standardized character of formal structures.

Library settings oriented toward the same occupational point of reference tend to employ similar technologies. Consistencies in work practices from one setting to another can be attributable to the common standards and principles from which those practices were derived. Occupational institutions provide a blueprint specifying how work is to be done. If these institutions could not be adopted verbatim, they provide at the very least a language and a system of logic that could be used to frame formal role expectations in the local setting. Because formalized expectations are not unique to one set of participants in one organization at one point in time, formal structure has the potential to be uniform across different organizations.

Occupational institutions form a common environment for libraries, an extraorganizational context that stabilizes the form of work arrangements. Local modifications of occupational practices are uniformly inhibited in settings collectively oriented toward the same occupational point of reference. Modification would be accepted only if it could be established that the change would be endorsed by the associations and schools that represent librarians, the dominant occupation in the task domain.[3] Changes would have to be seen to improve the "fit" between occupational institutions and local work arrangements. Work arrangements that are applications of a common institutional knowledge base would therefore tend to remain uniform across different settings.

In the survey, libraries were found to vary in the extent to which work was regulated by job descriptions and written records and in the degree to which consensus existed among the staff on the roles to be performed by library clerks and library assistants. Analyses of these data reveal that job descriptions, written records, and consensus tended to exist in those libraries collectively oriented toward the librarian occupation. Different libraries oriented toward the occupation tended to have similar role expectations and to have similar patterns of communication between those who provided reference and those who selected materials for acquisition. These role expectations and communication patterns reflected library association policies. Formalization appears to be one outcome of occupational control over work.

Notes

1. "An organization . . . which compiles its norms in written form is more formalized than one that does not. However, formalization should not be equated with the use of written norms" (Price, 1972, p. 107).

2. Occupational institutions enable individuals to understand their work by providing role expectations that apply in typical situations within a well-defined role-set. According to McHugh (1968:23–45), typicality, causal texture, and ontological necessity are properties of a "role-set" or relational basis of understanding. A librarian understands events in the library when he or she recognizes the correspondence between his or her current circumstances and the abstractly defined situations learned in library school. I assume that those in library work settings oriented towards library associations and schools are more likely to have

a relational sense of understanding of their work. I predict that the relational sense of understanding in these libraries is most compatible with job descriptions, written records, and other standardized work arrangements that correspond to occupational standards and principles.

McHugh contrasts "relativity" with a second basis of understanding he terms "emergence." Whereas a relational sense of understanding involves the application of an organized body of knowledge to practical tasks, an emergent sense of understanding is based on personal experiences, shared interpersonal experiences. While a relational sense of understanding would be associated with formalization, an emergent sense of understanding would be associated with informal work arrangements.

Informal role expectations are implicitly defined by norms in force among a particular set of individuals in particular settings. Understandings are inductively constructed from personal observations and recollections. The meaning of informal work arrangements would be fully understood only by those with uninterrupted experience in the setting with the personalities involved. The relevance of particular behaviors may be comprehensible only to those present at their inception. Registered as shared memories, expectations would be relatively implicit, leaving considerable room for revision and elaboration in the light of future events. Informal roles would be idiosyncratic to the particular locale and to individuals who participated in their creation and elaboration.

3. Weber (1947) classified organizations by the type of external agency that constructed the institutions: charismatic leaders, traditional figures in history, and rational-legal rule-making bodies. Each type of organization differed in its manner and capacity for changing rules.

6

Standardization

Libraries are relatively formal compared with other organizations that employ occupations in service activities at the technical level (Hall, 1968). Perhaps it is the use of standardized labels to describe personnel, tasks, and the location and timing of work activities that is indicative of this level of formalization. Consistency in language was quite apparent for "providing reference service" and "selecting new materials for acquisition." Informants within the same library setting interpreted questions predicated on these terms in a consistent fashion. Across different libraries, behavior associated with these terms seemed invariant. It was this degree of standardization that made a comparative survey of library work settings possible.

All the personnel in the settings visited could be identified in terms of one of five statuses: professional librarian, library assistant, library clerk, library technician, and subject area specialist. These categories seemed to be exhaustive. During the course of the investigation, no additional labels were suggested by informants. In most instances informants treated these statuses as mutually exclusive categories. However, in the course of the survey uncertainty was expressed in some libraries about the qualifications that distinguished each status. In most cases differences between the appropriate organizational classification and the appropriate occupational status seemed to account for the discrepancies. Despite these ambiguities, the same terminology was used across all the settings to label library personnel.

A consistent terminology existed for times and locations as well. The "reference desk" was typically the location from which most reference service was provided. Reference tasks were often organized in accordance with a posted schedule or timetable. Unlike reference tasks, the selection of materials for acquisition tended to be carried out at irregular times during temporarily slack periods. It was not associated with clearly defined locations, timetables, or deadlines.

Within library work settings, formalized structure took at least three forms. (1) Official documents: There were procedures that were officially documented as part of the administrative structure of the organization. (2) "Acknowledged" regulation: Personnel in many settings acknowledged the existence of "working" documents. For example, scratch pad records of the number and type of reference queries were often kept. Where official records of these transactions were also maintained, entries were often estimated from subtotals calculated from such running records. (3) Consensus on role expectations: Supplementing written norms were clearly recognized and mutually agreed on role expectations. Formalized work arrangements were associated with consensus on role expectations as well as with the existence of such artifacts as job descriptions, written instructions, and written records. Such role expectations and regulations stipulated standardized role relations among the categories of personnel and between those categories of personnel and the tasks performed in the work setting.[1] All three types of social control tended to be regarded as impersonal.

Formalization in these senses varied considerably from one library setting to another. Some operated with no evidence of written regulation. Respondents could not agree on the tasks that each occupational status was expected to perform. In other settings the table of organization was clearly spelled out and there was little confusion in the duties to be performed by each occupation. Thus despite the existence of standardized terminology across all library settings surveyed, the settings differed in the extent to which work arrangements were governed by explicit role expectations or written regulations and records.

Consensus on Occupational Role Expectations

Consensus on the assignment of specific tasks to members of an occupation is presumed to be the product of authoritative control in the work setting. Consensus on role expectations, as one measure of the explicitness of role expectations, is predicted to be positively associated with a collective orientation toward librarians and the library associations representing their interests. The standards and principles of librarianship articulated by those associations should provide a consistent set of role expectations regarding the capabilities and general responsibilities of library personnel. By providing a set of agreed on standards and by legitimizing the dominance order among library personnel, the institutions of librarianship should give such role expectations a more definite and distinct character.

Variations from One Library to Another

There is greater agreement on the role to be performed by each major occupational status than might have been expected, given the limited extent of regulation and documentation. Two members of a library's staff (one who regularly provided reference service and another who selected materials for acquisition on a regular basis) were questioned on occupational role expectations in their setting. Both were asked which combinations of selection and reference work would be regarded as objectionable conduct in their library work setting. By comparing the roles prescribed by each respondent, a measure of consensus of role expectations was obtained for each occupation. The greater the consensus among personnel, the more likely it would be that role expectations would be explicit.

With a few exceptions, there seemed to be complete agreement on the roles that professional librarians ought and ought not to perform in most libraries (82 percent of the libraries surveyed; see table 6-1). Although not quite as marked, consensus on role expectations for library clerks was also high in many libraries. In comparison, consensus on the role of library assistants varied extensively from one library to another. Library assistants are often given assignments and projects at the discretion of a librarian. In contrast to the duties of librarians and clerks, work performed by assistants seemed to vary from one time to another and from one assistant to another. These data imply that the responsibilities of assistants may be relatively irregular compared with the more routine responsibilities of clerks and librarians. Thus it appears that in most library settings librarians and clerks are subject to normative constraints of a different order than are assistants. Unanimously accepted role expectations would probably be supported by sanctions imposed by the workers themselves over and above any control exerted by their administrative superiors (Asch, 1958).

Occupational Orientations and Size

The Logic of the Analysis. Many readers may not be familiar with the logic of survey analysis or the tables employed to present survey results. Because the results of this study are important and contrary to popular and academic

Table 6-1
Consensus on Role Expectations among Regular Performers of Selection and Reference Tasks
(*percent*)

Consensus[a]	Professional Librarians	Library Clerks	Library Assistants
0 High	82	62	37
1	6	19	22
2	3	19	28
3	6	–	–
4	3	–	13
5	–	–	–
6 Low	–	–	–
Total, $N = 32$	100	100	100

[a] Disagreements were scored in the following fashion: desirable versus neutral, neutral versus objectionable were scored as 1; desirable versus objectionable was scored as 2.

impressions of the nature of occupations and organizations, I want everyone to assess the data that support the theoretical perspectives of this book. This section on the logic of the analysis and the next on reading the tables will enable readers to form their own conclusions about the results. Readers who are familiar with regression analysis may wish to skim these two sections.

Having access to the survey data, we can now examine the conditions under which consensus is most likely to occur. Of greatest interest is whether the more occupationally oriented libraries also have greater consensus on role expectations, as predicted. However, other factors may be expected to be associated with the level of consensus. In fact, consensus was negatively correlated with size and complexity. Consensus was lower in libraries with a larger number of positions that employed a greater number of different types of staff. In comparison, consensus was higher in smaller, less complex libraries. Reality tends to be a mixture of different processes in which no single factor accounts for all that is going on. In this case consensus appears to be the product of occupational orientations, size, and complexity.

The problem is to separate each of these factors so that we can see whether occupational orientations have an effect on consensus that is independent of the effects of size and complexity. We could use experimental procedures to address this problem. This would involve setting up libraries that varied in terms of their occupational orientations but were identical or constant in size and complexity. Then any variation from one library to another could not be associated with size and complexity because those variables are constants. Therefore if the variations in consensus were correlated with variations in occupational orientations, this association would exist independent of the size and complexity of the library. Of course, we could use experimental techniques to assess the independent effects of size by holding occupational orientations and complexity constant, and similarly for complexity. However, these procedures require the manipulation of people and organizations and the expenditure of large sums of money. Most studies in the social sciences use statistical procedures to discern the independent effects of several independent variables—for example, occupational orientations, size, complexity—on a dependent variable, such as consensus.

Regression analysis is employed in the study.[2] When the correlation (the connection or relationship) between occupational orientations and consensus is calculated, regression techniques statistically hold constant the effects attributable to variations in size and complexity. The effects of size and complexity on the correlation between occupational orientations and consensus are calculated and literally subtracted out. This is done simultaneously for each independent variable (when the correlation coefficients for size and for complexity as well as for occupational orientations are calculated). (See Mueller, Schuessler, and Costner, 1977, for a fuller discussion of statistics and regression analysis.)

The number of full-time positions and the number of occupational statuses were included in the statistical analyses as control variables because of their strong and explicable association with the dependent variable. Variables such as the size of circulation (negatively correlated with consensus on clerks) and the size of the acquisitions budget (positively correlated with consensus on clerks) were not included because the correlations were weak and statistically indistinct. Generally, the zero-order slope of a potential control variable had to be close to twice the size of its standard error before the variable was entered into the analysis (Duncan, 1966). If there was evidence that the zero-order association was suppressed by variables included in the analysis, this rule was modified.

Reading the Tables. Table 6-2 presents three regression analyses for consensus on library clerks, one for each relevant indicator of occupational orientations. As these variables are considered to be measures of same underlying concept, collective occupational orientations, a separate analysis was performed for each indicator. The fourth measure of collective occupational orientations, the coincidence of values and interests, was unrelated to consensus on role expectations. The first column Beta, presents the correlation coefficients. Beta can vary from -1.0 to 1.0, with -1.0 representing a perfect, negative correlation and 1.0 a perfect positive correlation between the variables. Positive and negative correlations that are close to zero indicate that no connection or relationship exists between the variables. If we look at the results of the first analysis, we can compare the correlations of three variables—awareness of specialist associations,

Table 6-2
Consensus on Role Expectations for Library Clerks as a Function of Collective Occupational Orientations

Independent Variables	Beta	Significance of Terms	R^2	Significance of Equations
Awareness of specialist associations	.298	.086	.269	.030
Number of positions	−.408	.026		
Number of statuses	−.144	.408		
Awareness of central associations	.361	.036	.307	.015
Number of positions	−.347	.044		
Number of statuses	−.090	.602		
Interest in professional librarians	.439	.008	.368	.005
Number of positions	−.442	.011		
Number of statuses	−.133	.407		

Note: $N = 32$. Control variables were the number of full-time positions and the number of occupational statuses. The dependent variable was consensus on role expectations for library clerks. See Reeves (1978, p. 250) for the correlation matrix of the independent, control, and dependent variables.

number of positions, and number of statuses—with consensus on library clerks. Most of the variation from one library to another is a function of the number of positions in a library (beta = −0.408). The level of awareness of specialist associations is positively related to the degree of role consensus (0.298) while variation in the number of statuses is only weakly correlated with consensus (−0.144). The association between complexity (number of statuses) and consensus was reduced or attenuated when the effect of size (number of positions) was subtracted out. When the indicator of occupational orientations is changed to awareness of central associations or to interest in professional librarians, the pattern of results is basically the same. The correlation between occupational orientations and consensus increases (from 0.298 to 0.361 and 0.439) while the effects due to size fluctuate (−0.408 to −0.347 and −0.442). But the correlations remain moderately strong and positive for occupational orientations and moderately strong and negative for size.

The third column, R^2, indicates the amount of the variation from one library to another that is accounted for by the three variables in each analysis. The first analysis could account for 26.9 percent of the variance; the second, 30.7 percent; and the third, 36.8 percent. Put another way, 73.1 percent of the variance remains unaccounted for in the first analysis, 69.3 percent in the second, and 63.2 percent in the third. Given all the information collected in the survey, I was unable to identify all the processes occurring in libraries that affect consensus. The R^2 gives some idea of the extent to which we can identify and hold all other relevant factors statistically constant.

While care has been taken to eliminate spurious effects by either statistically or procedurally holding constant other factors that affect consensus, all such factors have not been identified and controlled. Clearly, these results account for only a part of the reality experienced in library work settings.

The second and fourth columns report the significance of terms (the betas) and the significance of the equations (the overall results of each separate analysis). The notion of statistical significance is quite technical and is not critical to our understanding of the results.[3] Generally, it gives us some idea of the extent to which the results differ from those we might expect if the results were produced by chance alone—the smaller the number, the more certain we are that the results do not reflect chance. Within each analysis, the larger the correlation coefficient (beta), the smaller and more statistically significant the term. As each analysis is based on the same set of libraries ($N = 32$), the larger the "explained" variance (R^2), the smaller and more statistically significant the equation.[4]

When all factors associated with consensus are entered into the analysis, consensus on role expectations was found to be a function of the collective awareness of library associations (or interest in professional librarians as an occupational group) and the number of full-time positions. The arrows on figure 6-1 allow us to visualize the positive effect of occupational orientations

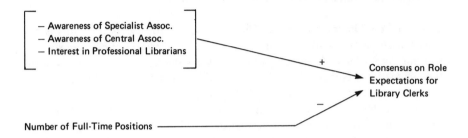

Collective Occupational
Orientations

— Awareness of Specialist Assoc.
— Awareness of Central Assoc.
— Interest in Professional Librarians

+

Consensus on Role
Expectations for
Library Clerks

−

Number of Full-Time Positions

Figure 6-1. Consensus on Role Expectations for Library Clerks as a Function of Collective Occupational Orientations and the Number of Full-Time Positions

and the negative impact of size on consensus. There is no arrow connecting occupational orientations and size because the correlation between these two factors was minimal (the occupational orientations of larger and smaller library settings were similar).

Consensus on Library Clerks. Consensus was related to three of the four indicators of occupational orientations. Consensus was somewhat more affected by variations in collective awareness of central associations than by that of specialist associations (beta = 0.361 versus beta = 0.298). The impact of the level of interest in professional librarians on consensus was greater than that for either measure of collective awareness of library associations. These results show that three of the four indicators of occupational orientation do have moderately strong, statistically independent, and positive effects on the level of one measure of formalization, consensus on role expection for library clerks.

The data indicate that it is the sheer number of positions, and not the complexity of internal operations, that adversely affected consensus on clerks. The size of the staff in the work settings sampled varied from a low of four positions, the arbitrarily set minimum, to twenty-seven. While the average (and median) number was eleven, one-third regularly employed only four or five people full-time, while one-eighth of the cases had over twenty positions.[5] Personnel in the thirty-two settings were identified as belonging to one of five occupational statuses: professional librarian, subject area specialist, library assistant, library technician, and library clerk. Only one setting employed all five. Eighty-one percent of the settings had only two or three statuses. Settings with a larger number of full-time positions tended to be the ones employing a greater variety of occupations. When both variables were introduced into the same regression analyses, the effect of the number of occupational statuses on consensus was reduced to virtually zero on each occasion.

Consensus on Library Assistants. The data analysis for library assistants is not nearly as straightforward as that for clerks. The number of occupational statuses was not correlated with consensus on library assistants. Two other measures of the occupational composition of a library—the presence of library assistants and the number of librarians as a proportion of total staff—were relevant.

The composition of the staff appeared to be related to the size and function of the library. Settings with more specialized holdings employed a few more people and often had library technicians or subject area specialists in addition to clerks and a librarian. Library assistants tended to be employed in larger, more complex settings. In the smaller libraries the general position of library assistant appeared to be supplanted by a more specialized combination of library clerks and library technicians or subject area specialists. While almost all settings employed at least one librarian (89 percent), only half employed two or more (56 percent). Librarians tended to constitute 11 to 20 percent of the staff in a work setting, but the percentage varied from this mode in about half of the cases. There was a tendency for the number of librarians to be related to the size of the acquisition's budget. In comparison, settings with higher circulations tended to have a greater proportion of librarians on staff. As the proportion of librarians was greatest in settings associated with universities, it seems that the educational qualifications of the senior library staff tend to mirror those of library users.

In addition, the size of circulation was also associated with consensus on library assistants. Using the number of volumes circulated in a year as an indicator of demand, the settings could be grouped into one of three categories: those with a circulation of fewer than 20,000 volumes, those with a circulation of more than 100,000 volumes, and those in between. The introduction of the size of the circulation and the proportion of librarians into the analyses was complicated by the fact that information on these new variables was not available for all thirty-two libraries. The problem of missing data was further complicated because, where data were available for one, they were often unavailable for the other, and vice versa. Records on circulation were not kept in some libraries. In many departmental work settings, figures were kept for the library as a whole, but not for the one department included in the survey. Some materials in most libraries did not circulate. The ratio of circulating to noncirculating material varied considerably from one setting to another. Some libraries had noncirculating collections. For these various reasons, comparable data were not available for ten of the thirty-two cases. The data necessary for calculating the proportion of librarians were obtained only after the survey instrument was revised. As a result, data were missing for eight cases. To maximize the number of cases included in the data analyses, two subsamples were drawn—one with complete information on circulation and the other with complete information on the proportion of librarians. Table 6-3 reports on the analyses that include the size of circulation as a variable, while the proportion or percentage of librarians is included in the analysis in table 6-4.

The three indicators of orientation that were associated with consensus on clerks were also related to consensus on assistants. Following the format outlined in table 6-2, three separate analyses were performed on the data, one for each indicator of occupational orientations. As tables 6-3 and 6-4 show, consensus on assistants was related to collective awareness of specialist associations more than to collective awareness of central associations, in direct contrast to the results for clerks. Awareness of specialist associations also had a greater effect on consensus than interest in professional librarians. In general, the coefficients representing the independent effects of occupational orientation on consensus were statistically a little less distinct for assistants than for clerks. See figure 6-2 for an illustration of these results.

For those cases for which data on the proportion of librarians are available (table 6-4), there tends to be more agreement on the roles to be performed by

Table 6-3
Consensus on Role Expectations for Library Assistants as a Function of Collective Occupational Orientations, Controlling for the Number of Materials Circulated

Independent Variables	Beta	Significance of Terms	R^2	Significance of Equations
Awareness of specialist associations	.440	.017	.586	.003
Number of positions	−.453	.059		
Circulation	−.065	.745		
Presence of library assistant	−.259	.173		
Awareness of central associations	.308	.136	.488	.017
Number of positions	−.361	.158		
Circulation	−.102	.651		
Presence of library assistant	−.202	.367		
Interest in professional librarian	.289	.120	.494	.017
Number of positions	−.338	.177		
Circulation	−.205	.344		
Presence of library assistant	−.303	.148		

Note: N = 22. Control variables were the number of full-time positions, the number of materials circulated, and the presence of assistants. The dependent variable was consensus on role expectations for library assistants. As in table 6-2, separate analyses were performed for each parallel indicator of occupational orientation. See Reeves (1978, p. 251) for the correlation matrix of the independent, control, and dependent variables.

Table 6-4

Consensus on Role Expectations for Library Assistants as a Function of Collective Occupational Orientations, Controlling for the Percentage of Professional Librarians

Independent Variables	Beta	Significance of Terms	R^2	Significance of Equations
Awareness of specialist associations	.376	.075	.485	.010
Number of positions	−.396	.077		
Percentage of professional librarians	.255	.218		
Presence of library assistants	−.345	.075		
Awareness of central associations	.271	.142	.456	.016
Number of positions	−.282	.172		
Percentage of professional librarians	.350	.081		
Presence of library assistants	−.318	.108		
Interest in professional librarian	.322	.066	.491	.009
Number of positions	−.256	.190		
Percentage of professional librarians	.423	.028		
Presence of library assistants	−.316	.100		

Note: N =24. The control variables were the number of full-time positions, the percentage of professional librarians, and the presence of library assistants. The dependent variable was consensus on role expectations for library assistants. See Reeves (1978, p. 252) for the correlation matrix of the independent, control, and dependent variables.

assistants in settings with a higher proportion of librarians and settings that do not hire library assistants. The second point is somewhat ironic—the presence of assistants on staff reduces the level of agreement among the staff concerning an assistant's duties. Role consensus is more easily attained when the expectations are only hypothetical. This fact may be yet another manifestation of the discretionary assignment of duties to assistants by librarians. Vagueness about role expectations emanating from this quarter may be reduced in settings with a higher ratio of librarians to nonlibrarians. In such circumstances librarians may have to devise among themselves more systematic procedures for assigning jobs to library assistants. Settings with a larger number of positions tended to employ library assistants and to hire fewer librarians as a proportion of the entire staff. When these variables are entered into the same analyses, the only consistent pattern that emerges among the control variables is that the presence of assistants in the setting exerts a negative effect on the level of consensus.

For the twenty-four libraries for which the percentage of librarians could be calculated, the presence of librarians in the library setting was positively associated with consensus on role expectations. Library settings with higher proportions of librarians were more likely to be collectively aware of specialist library associations. (This is represented by the curved, double-headed arrow in

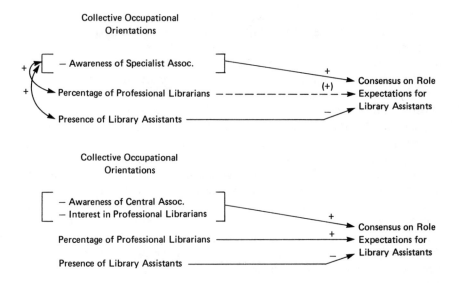

Figure 6-2. Consensus on Role Expectations for Library Assistants as a Function of Collective Occupational Orientations, the Percentage of Professional Librarians, and the Presence of Library Assistants

figure 6-2.) But collective awareness of central library associations or interest in the occupation was no greater in settings with a higher percentage of librarians than those with a lower percentage of librarians. (There is no double-headed arrow for these indicators in figure 6-2.) Comparison of the correlation coefficients in the three regression analyses on table 6-4 reveals that the independent effect of the presence of librarians was greater when awareness of central associations or interest in professional librarians represented occupational orientations (beta = 0.350 and 0.423, respectively). When awareness of specialist associations represented occupational orientations, the correlation coefficient was lowered (beta = 0.255). The presence of librarians seems to affect consensus on the role of library assistants, in part, by increasing collective awareness of specialist library associations. Settings with a higher percentage of librarians were more aware of specialist associations, and, in turn, settings that were more aware of specialist associations had greater consensus on library assistants. (The broken line in figure 6-2 represents that the percentage of librarians does not have a direct effect on consensus when the collective awareness of specialist associations is taken into account). The collective awareness of library associations mediated the effect of the presence of librarians on role consensus for library assistants.

The overall pattern of results in tables 6-2 to 6-4, regarding the effect of size on consensus is rather surprising. The literature on organizations suggests that bureaucratization, in response to greater size and complexity, should produce consensus on role expectations. Data showing positive correlations between indicators of formalization, size, and complexity are presented in a large number of studies. (In particular, see Child, 1972, and Hall, 1963, 1968.) The conventional wisdom on organizations is that increases in organizational size and complexity threaten the capacity of workers and supervisors to coordinate the flow of work. Bureaucratization is thought to arise in large part as a managerial response to this threat. Standardization of work is one of the mainstays of bureaucratization. Presumably, bureaucratization would improve, routinize, and regularize the flow of work by improving workers' consensus on their duties and obligations. According to this logic, we expect larger, more complex libraries to have greater role consensus because bureaucratization is more extensive in the larger, more complex libraries. The results in tables 6-2 to 6-4 are not consistent with either this reasoning or the correlations reported in the literature. Whether or not bureaucratic modes of control are devised to compensate for problems created by size and complexity, consensus on role expectations remains lower in larger library settings.[6]

Consensus on Librarians. With regard to the indicators of collective occupational orientations, the results regarding role consensus for librarians correspond to those regarding library clerks and assistants (the association is positive). However, because there was complete consensus on role expectations for librarians in over 80 percent of the library settings surveyed (see table 6-1), the data for librarians were not reported. The lack of variation from one library to another would make the results of a multivariate regression analysis unstable and therefore rather inconclusive.

Conclusion

With regard to the central hypotheses proposed in this study, the results are straightforward. Role consensus is a positive function of the occupational orientations of the work setting. Taken as a whole, these findings are consistent with the predictions that consensus on role expectations should be higher in occupationally oriented library settings.

The negative relationship between consensus and the number of positions suggests that the process that produces consensus is unlikely to involve managerial bureaucratization. Consensus on role expectations in library work settings is apparently related to occupational institutions and unrelated to processes of organizational administration qua organization. The presence of librarians is associated only with consensus on library assistants, and this relationship is mediated by the awareness of specialist library associations. Whether or not the presence of librarians is a factor, the collective occupational orientations among all members of the library staff, nonlibrarians and librarians alike, seems to have an important bearing on consensus on occupational role expectations.

Job Descriptions

The existence of job descriptions is a generally accepted indicator of formalization. Job descriptions acknowledged by these respondents were often associated with some form of official documentation, written procedures, or instructions. These measures constitute more conventional measures of formalization than consensus on role expectations. However, as in the case of consensus on role expectations, we would predict that libraries oriented toward the librarian occupation would be more likely to codify work arrangements. According to library association policies, librarians are expected to establish a formal system of control over the work carried out by nonlibrarians. The nonlibrarians' ignorance of the principles and standards of librarianship reinforces the duty of librarians to formally prescribe how nonlibrarians are to perform their jobs. As nonlibrarians are aware (and often reminded) of their ignorance of the principles and standards of librarianship, they are inclined to comply with formal regulations instituted by the librarian, the person acknowledged as possessing this requisite expertise.

Variations from One Library to Another

A number of measures of formalization were considered. The data reported in table 6-5 are based on information given by those who carried out reference work and selection on a regular basis. In each library two respondents—one who primarily provided reference, another who was engaged in selection—were asked to answer the questions listed in table 6-5. They were asked to indicate the degree to which each of the statements was a true description of the rules and understandings actually followed. In approximately 90 percent of the libraries, respondents reported that there were procedures to be followed. In two-thirds of the settings, most people did not make their own rules, but in at least three-quarters of the cases it was reported that people who worked together in that library devised their own particular work arrangements. The distinction seems to be between people as individuals and people as a group. Groups, not individuals, seemed to be able to establish work procedures. Complete job descriptions were reported to exist in a little less than 40 percent of the libraries. Thus, although procedures exist for most problems that arise in nearly all the libraries, these procedures probably consist of formal regulations in some settings and informally devised work arrangements in others.

In most respects official regulation is even less extensive than might have been anticipated from these results. Several measures of official documentation, reported by Inkson, Pugh, and Hickson (1970), were included in the survey of the initial seven settings. As these indicators were designed to measure the degree of formalization of large industrial firms, much of the terminology had to modified. Few, if any, libraries had a written statement of policy, general information booklets, terms of reference or job descriptions, or organizational

Table 6-5
**Formal Regulation Acknowledged by Regular Performers of Selection and
Reference Tasks, by Activity**

		Percentage of Library Settings	
Items	Response[a]	Reference	Selection
For most problems that arise, there are procedures to be followed	True, More true than false	91	88
Most people here make their own rules	False, More false than true	69	66
There are complete job descriptions covering these situations	True, More true than false	38	34
People who work together in this library devise their own particular work arrangements	False, More false than true	25	9

Note: $N = 32$.

[a]To avoid a response set, formalization was denoted by the responses True or More true than false for some items and by False or More false than true on the others.

charts. Discussions with library personnel revealed that some libraries had some written procedures or instructions regarding reference or selection and organized some sort of work schedules for these activities. There did not seem to be any consistent format for the latter two types of documents.

Questions about the presence of such documentation had to be formulated in such a way as to be meaningful and comparable from one setting to another. An activity was considered to be formal if it was explicitly mentioned in any written procedure. The person in charge of the library work in the setting was asked about the existence of written procedures or instructions. The results are reported in table 6-6. Written procedures or instructions describing reference or selection activities in some detail existed in fewer than 30 percent of the settings. The activities are mentioned in some explicit fashion in less than 40 percent of the cases. While there were slight variations between reference and selection in the extent to which they were subject to written procedures or instructions, the most striking finding was that neither activity was formally regulated in well over half of the libraries surveyed.

Job descriptions acknowledged by performers in the library work settings are more likely to be supported by official documentation as reported by the supervisor than vice versa. Where regular performers of selection acknowledged the existence of complete job descriptions for selection activities, some type of official documents existed in two-thirds of those settings (65 percent of complete job descriptions were supported by official written procedures or instructions; see table 6-7). Although the percentage was lower for reference

Table 6-6
Official Documentation Reported by the Person in Charge of the Library Setting, by Activity

		Percentage of Library Settings	
Items	Response	Reference	Selection
Are there written procedures or instructions which describe how these activities are to be performed	Activities described in some detail	13	29
	Activities explicitly mentioned	39	26
	Descriptions vague and implicit	48	45

Note: $N = 32$.

work, official procedures were also present in 58 percent of the settings where complete job descriptions were acknowledged to exist. In contrast, official procedures or instructions more often than not failed to be acknowledged by those who performed reference and selection work. Official procedures or instructions, where they did exist, were acknowledged as complete job descriptions in only 38 percent of the libraries.

A review of tables 6-5 to 6-7 reveals that job descriptions are not prevalent in the libraries surveyed. Written procedures or instructions were more often than not unknown or ignored by those who performed reference and selection activities. Nevertheless, in a number of libraries complete job descriptions were acknowledged to exist, and these job descriptions tended to be backed up by some form of official documentation. It now remains to be seen whether the more occupationally oriented libraries were the ones more likely to have instituted job descriptions.

A Complication: "Innovative" Library Settings

An initial inspection of the correlations between the indicators of occupational orientations and the existence of complete job descriptions revealed that the association was weak or nonexistent. A curvilinear relationship existed between occupational orientations and job descriptions. The curvilinearity was most pronounced for the measures of collective awareness of library associations. The relationship was strong and positive for those libraries with low to moderately high levels of collective awareness. (In comparison with libraries with low levels of awareness, libraries with moderately high levels of awareness tended to have job descriptions.) However, the relationship was slightly negative for those settings in which awareness of library associations was above average.

Table 6-7
**Asymmetrical Association between Formal Regulation Acknowledged by
Regular Performers of Selection and Reference and Official Documentation
Reported by the Person in Charge**
(*percent*)

Activity	Complete Job Descriptions Supported by Official Written Procedure or Instruction	Written Procedures or Instructions Acknowledged as Complete Job Descriptions
Selection	65	38
Reference	58	38

(In comparison with libraries with moderately high levels of awareness, libraries with the highest levels of awareness were slightly less likely to have job descriptions.)

In both cases four libraries were discovered to account for most of the curvilinearity. In these four libraries extensive awareness of library associations was combined with an extremely informal means of regulation. In one sense or another each one of these innovative libraries was a prototype or model library.[7] Three of the four might be classified as archives, their collections being unparalleled in the region and, perhaps, the nation. Each carried out functions peculiar to that library, functions that had been explicitly chartered or mandated by the provincial or federal governments. The chief librarians in two of the libraries had been elected to top executive positions in central library associations.

In terms of the background and contextual properties measured in the survey, innovative libraries were distinguished from others by the small number of their full-time positions, the virtual absence of library assistants, and their small circulations. They also differed in their level of collective awareness of library associations. The average scores on awareness for innovative libraries were over one standard deviation higher than the average scores for the other twenty-eight libraries in the sample. (the average score of the four innovative libraries was higher than approximately 85 percent of the twenty-eight other libraries). While their average scores for consensus on role expectations were over one standard deviation above the averages of the other twenty-eight libraries, the average scores on job descriptions for innovative libraries were over one standard deviation below the average for the other twenty-eight libraries. The former was as predicted; the latter was not. Innovative libraries eschewed all modes of formal regulation.

A dummy variable was set at 0 for innovative libraries and 1 for the more conventional libraries, and the measures of orientation were multiplied by this dummy variable. By this procedure interaction terms were created for each indicator of orientation. Every interaction term was more positively correlated with the use of job descriptions. The processes relating job descriptions and occupational orientations in conventional libraries appear to be quite different from those in innovative libraries. Conventional libraries seem to behave much as predicted, while innovative libraries seem to behave in exactly the opposite manner.

Occupational Orientations and the Size of Circulation

The existence of job descriptions for both activities is a positive function of occupational orientations and a negative function of the size of the circulation. The overall pattern of results is shown in figure 6-3. The size of the circulation and occupational orientations are positively correlated (represented by the curved, double-headed arrow in figure 6-3). In particular, the libraries with larger circulations were more likely to report that their values and interest coincided with those of the librarian occupation.

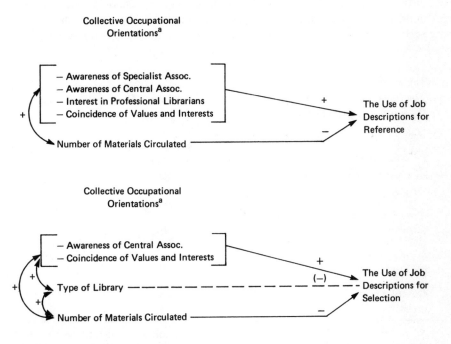

[a]Ranking innovative libraries as completely unoriented toward the occupation.

Figure 6-3. Use of Job Descriptions as a Function of Collective Occupational Orientations and the Number of Materials Circulated

The results for reference service are reported in table 6-8. All four indicators of occupational orientations are positively correlated with the use of job descriptions. As in the analysis of consensus on role expectations, a separate regression analysis was carried out for each measure of occupational orientations. While the magnitudes of the correlation coefficients vary from a low of 0.348 to a high of 0.649, the relationships are consistently positive no matter which indicator of occupational orientation is introduced into the analysis. Similarly, the effects of the size of the circulation are consistently negative. While occupational orientations favor the existence of job descriptions, the library's circulation appears to inhibit the use of job descriptions.

The pattern of results is somewhat the same for the selection of materials for acquisition. Only two measures of occupational orientation are associated with the use of job descriptions for this activity: the awareness of central library associations, and the extent to which the values and interests of the library coincide with those of the librarian occupation. Nevertheless, these two variables are both positively related to job descriptions.

A second property of the library was related to job descriptions for selection—the type of library. The type of library differentiates between library settings in terms of the extent to which the settings occupy a central position in the larger organization and the extent to which librarians occupy central positions of authority in the larger organization. The library settings were

Table 6-8
The Use of Job Descriptions for Reference Services as a Function of Collective Occupational Orientations

Independent Variables	Beta	Significance of Terms	R^2	Significance of Equations
Awareness of specialist associations[a]	.412	.054	.278	.046
Circulation	−.441	.041		
Awareness of central associations[a]	.483	.019	.346	.018
Circulation	−.414	.040		
Interest in professional librarian [a]	.348	.112	.230	.084
Circulation	−.434	.051		
Coincidence of values and interests[a]	.649	.008	.396	.008
Circulation	−.719	.008		

Note: $N = 22$. The control variable was the number of materials circulated. The dependent variable was job descriptions for reference service. See Reeves (1978, p. 255) for a correlation matrix of the independent, control, and dependent variables.

[a] Ranking innovative library settings as completely unoriented toward the occupation.

judged to vary widely on the central-peripheral dimension.[8] Table 6-9 classifies the library settings in terms of their intraorganizational centrality. Public libraries scored high, university and college libraries moderate, and business and government libraries low on the dimension of centrality. The library was considered to be a relatively peripheral department in business and government organizations, and the bible college. The goals and interests of the library as a library were clearly subordinated to the purposes and requirements of the larger organization. Library users within the larger organization tended to have a considerable effect on the determination of the type and level of library services that were provided. The autonomy of the librarian was restricted. In contrast, work settings in public libraries were far more central. Librarians in charge of these settings were far less likely to be subordinated to wishes of nonlibrarians. In public library systems with higher-level administrations, line administrators tended to be drawn from among the ranks of librarians. Most cases were judged to fall between these two extremes—the business and government libraries at one end of the scale and public library settings at the other. Settings attached to educational organizations or foundations were nominally subordinated to nonlibrary goals and policies. These libraries operated as one division in a confederated system rather than within a hierarchically ordered organization.

The type of library was correlated with the use of job descriptions. Government and business libraries were more likely to have job descriptions, while public libraries were less likely to be regulated in this fashion. However, public libraries tended to have larger circulations, and government or business libraries smaller circulations. (The positive correlation between library type and circulation is represented by a double-headed arrow in figure 6-3.) When the size of circulation is taken into account, we find that it is the size of the circulation,

Table 6-9
Intraorganizational Centrality by Type of Library

Intraorganizational Centrality	Type of Library (N)	Frequency	Percentage
High	Public (7) Professional (1) Legislative (1)	9	28.1
Moderate	University (5) College (5) Technical institute (2) Foundations (2)	14	43.8
Low	Government (6) Business (2) Bible college (1)	9	28.1
Total		32	100.0

not the type of library, that affects the use of job descriptions. (The broken line in figure 6-3 represents that the type of library does not have a direct effect on the use of job descriptions for the selection of materials. See table 6-10.)

Job descriptions may be considered to be artifacts that accrue through a process of sedimentation during the turnover of personnel. According to this imagery, collective procedures that have allowed a group to handle current events come to be accepted as informal group norms, as almost standard solutions to problems that they have encountered. These incipient norms may remain implicit and open-ended so long as the group is composed of individuals who have experienced these events together. For them, shared experience provides the basis for unstated agreement on current norms. The arrival of newcomers or, in the case of this study, the arrival of new members to the library staff is problematic. Not being privy to the historical events that spawned these informal understandings, new members of staff must be told how things are to be done. In lieu of shared experience, existing staff must translate their unstated normative understandings into explicit regulations that can be communicated to newcomers. When explaining the import of these regulations, they have to emphasize their systemic purposes rather than their personal significance.

"Old-timers" can maintain some semblance of their personal understandings only by enforcing the more explicit regulations in their dealings with the newcomers. In turn, the newcomers hold the others to these explicit regulations.[9]

Table 6-10
The Use of Job Descriptions for the Selection of Materials as a Function of Collective Occupational Orientations

Independent Variables	Beta	Significance of Terms	R^2	Significance of Equations
Awareness of central associations[a]	.390	.061	.348	.048
Circulation	−.356	.105		
Type of library	.277	.205		
Coincidence of values and interests[a]	.527	.037	.378	.033
Circulation	−.592	.021		
Type of library	.307	.156		

Note: N = 22. The control variables were the number of materials circulated and intra-organizational centrality. The dependent variable was job descriptions for the selection of materials. In Reeves (1978) the type of library is represented by the variable intraorganizational dependency, which is the inverse of intraorganizational centrality. Thus the signs of the correlations have been reversed. See Reeves (1978, p. 255) for the correlation matrix of the independent, control, and dependent variables.

[a]Ranking innovative libraries as completely unoriented toward the occupation.

The previously informal understandings come to be deposited as formal task descriptions. Each time that a newcomer replaces an experienced member of staff, a new layer of job descriptions, formulated from the understandings that had emerged in the interim, are laid down. At any point in time, then, the formal job descriptions in a library work setting represent the sedimented artifacts that have accumulated with successive turnovers in staff.

According to this line of reasoning, job descriptions would be acknowledged and taken into account by those working in the setting if the job descriptions are consistent representations of the systematic intercontingencies apparent to newcomers, and if they correspond to local history as experienced by the old-timers. There are at least two languages that could accomplish the translation of history into a system of regulation: terminology associated with the institutions of librarianship and library science, and terminology associated with the institutions surrounding the goals and policies of the library as an organization. (See, for example, Clark, 1972, on the organizational "saga".) To the extent that library job descriptions are rationalized in terms of principles and standards of librarianship already known to newly recruited staff, the structure of organizational norms would be more immediately comprehensible to them. Occupational orientations as measured by collective awareness of library associations and the coincidence of values and interests between the library and the occupation indicate that at least one relevant institutionalized language would be available to accommodate a process of sedimentation.

Formalization associated with a process of sedimentation may be disrupted by extensive contact with library users. To ensure that potential clients use library services, library staff frequently have to familiarize patrons with the available services and teach them the procedures that must be followed in order to obtain those services. This process of mobilization is somewhat akin to the process of formal co-optation identified by Selznick (1949, pp. 13-14). For staff members the role of accommodating or instructing clients accounts for a greater proportion of their duties in libraries with relatively large circulations. In comparison to business and government libraries, which serve relatively small numbers of clients (executives, research workers, and technical experts), public libraries cater to a much larger clientele, many of whom are not familiar with library procedures or services. In public libraries it may be very difficult to deal successfully with library users and at the same time comply fully with formal job descriptions. Client-oriented arrangements may not fit well with sedimented task descriptions. In the press of events arrangements worked out with particular patrons may take precedence over job descriptions and may debureaucratize the work setting.

In their article on bureaucracy in social service agencies in Israel, Katz and Eisenstadt (1960) argued that work setting contacts with clients, especially clients unfamiliar with available services and procedures, created role conflicts for workers that tended to debureaucratize those governmental agencies. They found that mobilizing and instructing clients led to deviations from formally defined job requirements. The results in tables 6-8 and 6-10 are consistent with this interpretation. The size of circulation is consistently associated with the relative absence of job descriptions.

Controlling for the size of circulation in the regression analyses revealed a much stronger association between job descriptions and measures of occupational orientations. Libraries with large circulations tended to be most oriented toward the occupation, with innovative libraries ranked as completely unoriented toward the occupation. (A double-headed arrow represents this correlation in figure 6-3). On the one hand, the occupational orientations of these settings provided a basis for sedimenting job descriptions; on the other, their extensive circulations inhibited this same process. These two factors tended to cancel each other's effects. In particular, the effects of the coincidence of interests and values on job descriptions were almost entirely suppressed by the effects associated with the size of circulation. The strength of both processes became apparent only when regression analysis was used to isolate the effects of each factor independent of the effects of the other.

Conclusion

The existence of job descriptions for selection or reference work is positively associated with normative orientations toward librarians and the associations that represent their interests. The presence of librarians was not a factor. Regardless of the numbers or the percentage of librarians on staff, settings more oriented toward the occupation were more likely to have job descriptions. The correlation between occupational orientations and job descriptions was only clearly apparent when the size of circulation was controlled. Larger circulations tended to debureaucratize library operations by reducing reliance on job descriptions. Because occupationally oriented libraries tended to be the ones with larger circulations, these two effects worked in opposite directions— higher occupational orientations fostered job descriptions and higher circulations eroded job descriptions. Although this suppression effect makes it difficult for an observer to detect either relationship, regression analysis revealed the independent effects of each factor, showing that both occupational orientations and size of the circulation were strong correlates of job descriptions.

One other complication made it difficult to discern the relationship between occupational orientations and job descriptions. These results are typical only for normal or noninnovative libraries. Four innovative settings in the sample of thirty-two libraries were discovered to be most aware of library associations and, at the same time, most unwilling to institute job descriptions in accordance with the policies of those associations. The rationale that was given was that standard library procedures were not appropriate for their particular library, given their library's mandate to develop a special collection and provide unique services in the region. These libraries displayed high levels of role consensus, as predicted, but they purposefully avoided job descriptions to codify their operations. This occurred for written records as well as for job descriptions.

Written Records

We would predict that written records as well as job descriptions would be associated with occupational orientations. Library association policies clearly require a librarian to establish a hierarchical and formal system of control over library work. Written records would complement job descriptions by providing a check on whether work was being carried out in the manner prescribed by the librarian. Most library hours are such that the supervising librarian would not be able to personally supervise the work being done by nonlibrarians on staff.

Variations from One Library to Another

Written records, at least those bearing on selection and reference work, were common in less than half of the libraries surveyed. Table 6-11 reports on data comparable to those in table 6-5. In each library setting, a regular performer of reference tasks and a regular performer of selection tasks were asked to answer the question listed in table 6-11. They were asked to indicate the degree to which a statement was a true description of the rules and understandings actually followed. Written records for selection were acknowledged to exist in the little over a third of the settings, while the percentage is only marginally higher for reference service.

Some libraries attempted to schedule these activities and keep track of them on some official basis. When they existed, work schedules seemed to

Table 6-11
Formal Regulation Acknowledged by Regular Performers of Selection and Reference, by Activity

		Percentage of Library Settings	
Item	Response	Reference	Selection
This library keeps a written record of everyone's performance	True, More true than false	38	34

Note: N =32.

be consistently associated with some type of recordkeeping. The person in charge of the work setting was asked about the frequency with which entries were made in official records. The frequency with which records were updated was presumed to measure the degree to which work was scheduled on a detailed, formal basis. The results are reported in table 6-12. No official records were maintained for reference services rendered in one half of the cases. Fully 83 percent of the cases had no official records on the selection of materials. In many of these settings records were kept on the clerical process of ordering materials but not on the judgmental process—the selection of materials—that preceded the placement of those orders. The widespread absence of official records seems to match the equally pervasive lack of written procedures or instructions reported in table 6-6. Where these activities were subject to any official documentation, reference services tended to be regulated by a system of recordkeeping, while selection tended to be governed by written procedures.

A comparison of the incidence of written records and official records showed that written records acknowledged by regular performers of reference and selection were often backed up by some form of official record. For example, where regular performers of reference work acknowledged the existence of written records for reference activities, those records took the form of official, ongoing logs in all but one case (86 percent of written records were supported by official records). However, the reverse did not hold true; official records were often not acknowledged as written records. The results in table 6-13 parallel those for job descriptions in table 6-7. The written procedures or official recordkeeping reported by those in charge in many cases seemed to be merely on the books and ignored in the work setting. The statistical relationship between acknowledged regulation and official documentation is asymmetrical, with the latter giving substance to the former, rather than vice versa.

Table 6-12
Official Documentation Reported by the Person in Charge of the Library Setting, by Activity

		Percentage of Library Settings	
Item	Response	Reference	Selection
If this library keeps track	On-going log	38	8
of how activities are carried	Daily	0	0
out, how frequently are	Weekly	4	0
records updated?	Monthly	0	4
	Yearly	8	4
	Personal records only	4	29
	No records kept	46	54

Note: $N = 24$.

Table 6-13
Asymmetrical Association between Formal Regulation Acknowledged by
Regular Performers of Selection and Reference and Official Documentation
Reported by the Person in Charge
(*percent*)

Activity	Written Records Supported by Official Records	Official Records Acknowledged as Written Records
Selection	56	38
Reference	86	50

Occupational Orientation and the Size of the
Acquisitions Budget

The use of written records to regulate reference work appears to be a product of an occupational component, represented by the collective awareness of library associations, and an organizational component, represented by the size of the acquisitions budget. The budget for acquisitions was the only budget for which comparable data existed in all thirty-two libraries. Over one-half of the settings had acquisition budgets of $40,000 or less (Canadian dollars, 1973), although one-quarter had budgets in excess of twice that amount. Figure 6-4 presents a schematic representation of the results reported in table 6-14.

The size of the acquisitions budget has both a direct and an indirect effect on the use of written records in reference work. In terms of the direct effect, the size of the budget is indicative of the social support that exists for the library and the services it provides to its clientele and the public at large. The greater financial support received by a library, the more likely it is that the library uses some system of accounting on a regular basis. Records of reference services rendered by the library provide tangible evidence of the practical value of acquisitions purchased with past budget allotments. These statistics can be used to justify past expenditures and legitimate requests for additional funding in the future. The size of the acqustions budget also has an indirect effect on written records by increasing the collective awareness of library associations. Libraries with larger budgets tend to be more aware of library associations, especially the central library associations, while libraries with smaller budgets are relatively less aware of these associations. (This positive correlation is represented by the curved, double-headed arrow on figure 6-4.) The standards of library service are more relevant in libraries with larger budgets. The principles of library administration outlined by library associations provide a rationale for the formal regulation of library work, in particular, for the establishment of records and statistics on library operations. By following and implementing

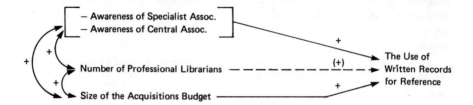

^aRanking innovative libraries as completely unoriented toward the occupation.

Figure 6-4. Use of Written Records for Reference as a Function of Collective Occupational Orientations and the Size of the Acquisitions Budget

Table 6-14
The Use of Written Records for Reference Services as a Function of Collective Occupational Orientations

Independent Variables	Beta	Significance of Terms	R^2	Significance of Equations
Awareness of specialist associations[a]	.332	.067	.410	.002
Acquisitions budget	.395	.026		
Number of professional librarians	.054	.768		
Awareness of central associations[a]	.303	.072	.407	.002
Acquisitions budget	.341	.063		
Number of professional librarians	.167	.322		

Note: $N = 32$. The control variables were the size of the acquisitions budget and the threshold number of professional librarians. The dependent variable was written records for reference service. See Reeves (1978, p. 254) for the correlation matrix of the independent, control, and dependent variables.

[a]Innovative library settings are scored as completely unoriented toward the occupation.

occupational standards of practice, well-funded libraries can neutralize any questions that may be raised about the adequacy or the appropriateness of library procedures.

The effects of the third factor, the presence of librarians on staff, are mediated both by the collective awareness of library associations and by the size of the acquisitions budget. Libraries that have larger budgets are more aware of library associations and have greater numbers of librarians. With regard to the size of the budget, either well-funded libraries employ more librarians or libraries with many librarians succeed in obtaining greater financial support. In either event it is the size of the budget not the number of librarians that is associated with the use of written records. The presence of librarians seems to contribute only indirectly to occupational standards of practice by orienting others in the work setting toward the librarian occupation.

This finding gives a clue as to how occupational standards are instituted in practice. Occupational standards are not implemented through the personal conduct of each individual librarian, with greater numbers of individual librarians adding up to more pervasive occupational work arrangements. Librarians do not rely on force of numbers in the work setting to compel others to comply with occupational standards against their will. Rather, librarians appear to affect library work arrangements by influencing the normative climate in the work setting. It is only when an awareness of library associations is shared by nonlibrarians as well as librarians that the policies of these associations become a source of authority that legitimizes the use of written records to monitor reference work. The presence of two or more librarians creates a concrete reference group in the work setting that increases the visibility and relevance of library association policies for others and thus enables librarians to implement some occupational standards of practice.

This argument applies only to noninnovative library settings. The positive association between the use of written records and a collective awareness of library associations occurs only among noninnovative settings. Exclusion of the innovative settings from this analysis has the effect of increasing the magnitude of the positive correlation between the number of librarians and the collective awareness of library associations. In this event the mediating effect of collective awareness on the statistical relationship between the number of librarians and the use of written records is if anything more pronounced than the effect reported in tables 6-14 and 6-15.

As with reference work, written records tend to regulate the selection of materials in library settings with large acquisitions budgets and several librarians. When collective awareness of specialist associations is the indicator of orientation, the pattern of results is very similar to those obtained for reference service. However, the pattern of results is quite different when collective awareness of central associations represents occupational orientations in the regression analysis. The effects of both the numbers of librarians and the size of the acquisitions budget are mediated by the collective awareness of central library associations. The occupation is the sole source of formal regulation for the selection of material for acquisition. For this more professional task the size of the acquisitions budget and the presence of librarians may indirectly affect work arrangements by increasing the awareness of central library associations. It seems that the occupation is the sole source of authority for instituting written records for the selection of materials for acquisition.

Table 6-15

The Use of Written Records for the Selection of Materials as a Function of Collective Occupational Orientations

Independent Variables	Beta	Significance of Terms	R^2	Significance of Equations
Awareness of specialist associations[a]	.369	.060	.308	.015
Acquisitions budget	.304	.105		
Number of professional librarians	−.012	.953		
Awareness of central associations[a]	.392	.030	.337	.008
Acquisitions budget	.223	.242		
Number of professional librarians	.108	.543		

Note: N = 32. The control variables were the size of the acquisitions budget and the threshold number of professional librarians. The dependent variable was written records for the selection of materials. See Reeves (1978, p. 254) for the correlation matrix of the independent, control, and dependent variables.

[a]Innovative library settings are scored as completely unoriented toward the occupation.

This argument, like the one regarding the number of librarians, applies only to noninnovative library settings. The positive association between the use of written records and a collective awareness of library association occurs only among noninnovative settings. If the innovative settings were excluded from the analysis, the correlation between the size of the acquisitions budget and a collective awareness of central associations is unaffected (although the correlation would be reduced for a collective awareness of specialist associations). The results reported in table 6-15 and summarized in figures 6-4 and 6-5 would be essentially the same if the four innovative settings were not included in the analysis.

Conclusions

Written records, like consensus on role expectations and job descriptions, are functions of occupational orientations. In particular, the awareness of library associations was critical for written records. As with job descriptions, these results are typical of noninnovative libraries only. While the four innovative libraries identified in the sample of thirty-two were most aware of library associations and displayed a high level of consensus on occupational role expectations, they shunned job descriptions and written records modeled on standard library association prescriptions. However, the predicted pattern of results held true for the other twenty-eight libraries in the survey.

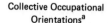

Collective Occupational
Orientations[a]

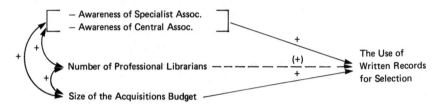

[a]Ranking innovative libraries as completely unoriented toward the occupation.

Figure 6-5. Use of Written Records for Selection as a Function of the Collective Awareness of Central Library Associations

The direct (independent) effect of the presence of librarians on standardization of library operations has consistently been reduced when collective awareness of central or specialist library associations is taken into account in the regression analyses. The number of librarians indirectly affects the use of written records by increasing the collective awareness of both types of associations. Earlier, we found that the percentage of librarians indirectly influences role consensus on library assistants by enhancing the collective awareness of specialist associations. The effect of the presence of librarians has always been mediated by occupational orientations toward library associations. Mere strength of numbers in the work setting does not enable librarians to standardize library work arrangements. These results emphasize the importance of library associations and collective occupational orientations. When instituting formal mechanisms of control in libraries, librarians appear to rely on both the normative foundations established by library associations and the endorsement of nonlibrarians in the work setting.

The use of written records was also positively related to the size of the acquisitions budget. This finding seems to contradict earlier results. Consensus was a negative function of the number of full-time positions and job descriptions were negatively associated with the size of the library's circulation. This suggests that these indicators of size actually measure different properties or aspects of a library's operation. The size of the acquisitions budget represents the extent of external financial support for the library (the library's legitimacy in the larger society). The size of circulation measures the extent of external operations, the number of transactions between the library and its clientele. The number of full-time positions reflects the size of the library's internal operations. Settings with greater numbers of personnel tended to satisfy higher levels of demand from their clientele. Although settings with larger acquisitions budgets tended also to have larger staffs, there was no relationship between the size of the acquisition budget and the size of circulation. While more legitimate libraries are more likely to institute some measure of formal control in the form of written records, libraries with larger internal or external operations are less likely to have job descriptions or consensus on role expectations. Unlike the measures of occupational orientation, no single indicator or organizational size was correlated with consensus, job descriptions, and written records. Size per se has no single or simple relationship with standardization in library work settings.[10]

"Professional" versus "Nonprofessional" Role Expectations

If authoritive control in library work settings is occupationally based, the particular tasks assigned to each occupation should reflect the principles and standards of librarianship. In library settings collectively oriented toward the librarian occupation, role expectations for occupational statuses did tend to model standards of librarianship outlined by central library associations. According to those institutions, a professional librarian may specialize, carrying out only some of the activities performed by librarians. One librarian could specialize in the selection of materials, a second in reference service, while a third performed some combination of those two activities. Librarians are not all expected to perform an identical set of duties. They tended to have greater latitude vis-à-vis the possible organization of work arrangements, including the possibility of assigning different duties to members of the same occupation.

With respect to the position of library assistants, the institutions of librarianship are more ambiguous. On the one hand, library assistants are regarded explicitly as nonprofessionals. As such, they are excluded from participating in the selection of materials for acquisition. On the other hand, library assistants are regarded implicitly as almost understudies, paraprofessionals assisting librarians in the conduct of their professional duties. In this capacity it might be possible for a library assistant to become involved in a professional activity such as selection. Role expectations in many settings reflected this ambiguity in occupational standards, allowing the possibility but not the necessity of library assistants' performing selection as well as reference tasks.

It would be predicted that role expectations permitting latitude for specialization among librarians would tend to exist in library settings oriented toward the librarian occupation. It is not as easy to predict the results for library assistants. The data in this section indicate that settings oriented toward the same occupational point of reference have similar role expectations for librarians and library assistants. In particular these role prescriptions are more likely to permit intraoccupational specialization among librarians and among assistants, as predicted.

The Possibility of Intraoccupational Specialization

If members of the same occupation could perform different sets of tasks without violating role expectations in the work settings, the possibility for intraoccupational specialization was considered to be high.[11] For example, if one member of an occupation only selected materials for acquisition, while another only provided reference service, and yet another did both (S, or R, or S & R), the possibilities for intraoccupational specialization would be unlimited. The various combinations of reference and selection are ranked in table 6-16 from high to low with respect to the number of alternative roles that may be performed. The possibilities for intraoccupational specialization vis-à-vis selection and reference tasks were unlimited for librarians and for assistants in 19 percent of the libraries and in 6 percent of the cases for clerks. Where two of the three alternatives could be exercised, specialization among librarians was frequently accomplished by making the less professional of the two activities, reference, optional. (The pattern of role expectations in five of the eight settings was S, or S & R—all, some, or none of the librarians may perform reference in addition to selection.) In contrast, it was the selection task that was typically considered optional for assistants and clerks. (The pattern of expectations was "R, or S & R" in six of seven settings and three of five settings, respectively.) Overall, latitude for intraoccupational specialization existed in over 40 percent of the settings for both librarians and assistants, while such possibilities existed for clerks only 22 percent of the time.

Professional Librarians. The contrast for librarians was between specialist conceptions and generalist expectations of the librarian. As generalists, librarians would be expected to carry out most of the tasks performed in the work setting. They were always expected to perform both reference and selection activities where role prescriptions confined librarians to one course of action. Heydebrand (1973, p. 183, fn. 26) stated that "generalist professionals are likely to share at least some functions with others resulting in some overlap of tasks, i.e., it implies the 'local' orientation of the home guard among [generalist] professionals." The implication is that specialist professionals may be oriented less toward the employing organization and, possibly, more toward their occupation and its institutions. Heydebrand was referring to the orientation of individual professionals rather than to the collective orientations of the setting within which they worked. Nevertheless, because there was a close relationship between individual occupational orientations and the collective orientations of others with whom they worked, settings with specialist conceptions of the librarian should presumably be the ones which were collectively oriented toward the occupation.

Role expectations that permit intraoccupational specialization appear to reflect diffuse occupational institutions. Specialist role conceptions are sponsored

Table 6-16
The Possibility of Intraoccupational Specialization among Professional
Librarians, Library Assistants, and Library Clerks
(*percent*)

		Occupation		
Specialization	Variety of Task Assignments within the Occupation	Professional Librarians	Library Assistants	Library Clerks
High	Three options	19	19	6
S and R, plus S only, and R only[a] (one composite pattern)		(6)	(6)	(2)
Moderate	Two options	25	22	16
S and R, plus S only[b]		(5)	(1)	(1)
S and R, plus R only		(3)	(6)	(3)
S only, plus R only (three composite patterns)		(0)	(0)	(1)
Low	No options	56	59	78
S and R[c]		(18)	(11)	(4)
S only		(0)	(0)	(1)
R only		(0)	(5)	(13)
Neither S nor R (four composite patterns)		(0)	(3)	(7)
Total		100	100	100
		(32)	(32)	(32)

Note: Frequencies are given in parentheses. Where several patterns of role expectations have similar scores on specialization (where specialization is moderate or low), the frequencies are provided for each pattern.

[a]S and R, plus S only, and R only: Some could do both selection and reference, some could do selection only, and some could do reference only.

[b]S and R, plus S only: Some could do both selection and reference, and some could do selection only.

[c]S and R: All are expected to do both selection and reference.

by both central and specialist library associations. The data indicate that the possibility of intraoccupational specialization is as likely to be associated with the collective awareness of central associations as the collective awareness of specialist associations (beta = 0.335 and beta = 0.298, respectively). The results reported in table 6-17 are summarized by the diagram in figure 6-6.

Generalist role expectations were typically found in the larger and more complex library work settings—the settings that employed library assistants and library clerks. The relationships between role prescriptions for librarians, on the one hand, and the number of full-time positions and the number of occupations, on the other, were attenuated when the presence of library assistants was

Table 6-17
Specialist Role Expectations for Professional Librarians as a Function of Collective Occupational Orientations

Independent Variables	Beta	Significance of Terms	R^2	Significance of Equations
Awareness of specialist associations[a]	.298	.081	.540	.001
Number of positions	−.052	.765		
Number of statuses	−.097	.524		
Presence of library assistants	−.569	.002		
Presence of library clerks	−.426	.004		
Awareness of central associations[a]	.335	.028	.571	.000
Number of positions	−.002	.989		
Number of statuses	−.067	.652		
Presence of library assistants	−.559	.001		
Presence of library clerks	−.440	.003		

Note: $N = 32$. The control variables were the number of full-time positions, the number of occupational statuses, the presence of library assistants, and the presence of library clerks. The dependent variable was the possibility of specialization among professional librarians. See Reeves (1978, p. 259) for the correlation matrix of the independent, control, and dependent variables.

[a]Ranking innovative library settings as completely unoriented toward the occupation.

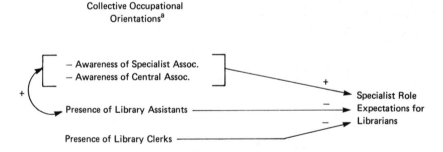

[a]Ranking innovative libraries as completely unoriented toward the occupation.

Figure 6-6. Specialist Role Expectations for Librarians as a Function of Collective Occupational Orientations, the Presence of Library Assistants, and the Presence of Library Clerks

statistically taken into account. It is the presence of subordinate occupations, assistants and clerks, that seemed to encourage generalist rather than specialist expectations. The feeling that a librarian should be involved with all aspects of library operations may be part of the expectation that a librarian, as an administrator, must supervise work done by untrained support staff (assistants and clerks).

Occupational institutions may be providing an impetus toward increasing the division of labor in libraries. Occupational institutions articulated by library associations outside the library may be a source of differentiation within library work settings. Institutionalized definitions of work typically prescribed an idealized system of action, incorporating all conceivable categories of personnel and clients as well as every conceivable type of activity that may be carried out in the task domain. This idealized system is generally more elaborate than any existing organizational division of labor. However, as a library develops organizational structures in accordance with the idealized system outlined in the policies of library associations, one would expect the division of labor to increase as the library incorporates a greater diversity of personnel, clients, and tasks into its work arrangements.[12] In fact, specialist role expectations are more likely to exist in occupationally oriented libraries. Because role expectations that permit a greater specialization among librarians may not be acted on to create an actual division of labor in the work setting, we must take care not to impute too much when interpreting these data. This finding is nevertheless intriguing.

Library Assistants. Role expectations for library assistants tended to mirror those for librarians. The pattern of results in figure 6-7 and table 6-18 are very similar to those for librarians. The correlation between specialist role expectations for the two occupations was high. As with librarians, administrative considerations seemed to limit the possibilities for specialization among library assistants. Library assistants were restricted in the kinds of roles that they

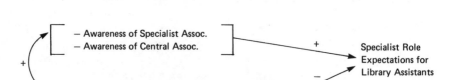

Collective Occupational
Orientations[a]

[a]Ranking innovative libraries as completely unoriented toward the occupation.

Figure 6-7. Specialist Role Expectations for Library Assistants as a Function of Collective Occupational Orientations and the Presence of Library Assistants

could perform in settings with a relatively large number of different occupations, the settings that tended to employ assistants. Statistically controlling for the presence of assistants reduced the effects of organizational complexity (see table 6-18). Because the presence of library assistants suppressed the effects of occupational orientation, controlling for the presence of library assistants also had the effect of revealing a relationship between specialist expectations for assistants and the collective awareness of library associations.

Expectations regarding library assistants are affected by two contradictory sets of considerations. The policy statements of the ALA explicitly recognize the administrative position of the assistant. In theory, professional librarians may delegate many of their supervisory duties to assistants. The library assistant occupies a position of authority in libraries analogous to that of the noncommissioned officer in military organizations. Assistants generally exercise authority over library clerks and library technicians, an authority delegated to them by librarians. It is in their capacity as administrators that assistants may become involved in the selection of materials for acquisition, that is, they may come to be regarded as generalists.

However, according to occupational institutions, library assistants are also regarded as nonprofessionals. As such, they should be explicitly excluded from the selection of materials for acquisition. Selection should be carried out solely by qualified librarians. Role expectations requiring assistants to participate in the selection process may reflect administrative realities, but they contravene occupational standards. Conversely, expectations prohibiting assistants from selecting materials may be unrealistic from an administrative point of view. The nonprofessional status of library assistants conflicts with their administrative status as generalists.

Table 6-18
Specialist Role Expectations for Library Assistants as a Function of Collective Occupational Orientations

Independent Variables	Beta	Significance of Terms	R^2	Significance of Equations
Awareness of specialist associations[a]	.387	.032	.363	.005
Number of statuses	−.232	.161		
Presence of library assistants	−.486	.010		
Awareness of central associations[a]	.351	.044	.351	.006
Number of statuses	−.211	.216		
Presence of library assistants	−.417	.018		

Note: N = 32. The control variables were the number of occupational statuses and the presence of library assistants. The dependent variable was the possibility of specialization among library assistants. See Reeves (1978, p. 259) for the correlation matrix of the independent, control, and dependent variables.

[a]Ranking innovative library settings as completely unoriented toward the occupation.

Table 6-19

Role Expectations for Library Assistants as a Function of Their Presence

Role Expectations	Presence	Absence
Selection required		
(S and R)	8	3
Library assistants as generalists	(54)	(18)
Selection prohibited		
(R only; neither R nor S)	5	3
Library assistants as nonprofessionals	(33)	(18)
Selection optional		
(S, R, S and R; R, S and R)	2	11
Library assistants as paraprofessionals	(13)	(64)
Total	15	17

Note: Percentages are in parentheses.

From the regression analysis in table 6-18, we know that the possibility for specialization among library assistants is more conceivable in their absence when the issue is hypothetical. Specialist role expectations give library assistants a paraprofessional status. As table 6-19 shows, specialist or paraprofessional expectations occur in 64 percent of the settings without library assistants, as opposed to only 13 percent of the settings with library assistants. Where specialization among librarians is not permitted, library assistants may be regarded as either nonprofessionals or as generalists. Generalist role expectations exist in 54 percent of the settings with library assistants, as opposed to 18 percent of the settings without them.

Table 6-20 investigates the pattern of behavior associated with these role expectations in the fifteen settings employing library assistants. Where assistants are expected to be generalists, in every case the reported behavior of library assistants violates occupational standards vis-à-vis the selection of materials. In comparison, in those settings in which assistants are regarded as nonprofessionals or paraprofessionals (four of seven settings), the behavior of library assistants tends to correspond to those standards. With regard to specialist or paraprofessional role expectations, all possible role options are not necessarily exercised in practice. While generalist role expectations clearly violate the intent of occupational institutions, it is not as clear that specialist or paraprofessional expectations do so in practice.

Those who are concerned that library assistants may be performing a "professional" task that should be reserved for librarians must find these results disquieting. It is not at all clear that this "problem" is due to the press of administrative necessity in the work setting. It is true that library assistants are more likely to be regarded as generalists in the libraries that employ them. In these libraries both the behavior of library assistants and role expectations regarding

Table 6-20
The Behavior of Library Assistants as a Function of Role Expectations

	Role Expectations		
Behavior	Generalist[a]	Nonprofessional[b]	Paraprofessional[c]
No one listed as selecting materials	0 (0)	3 (60)	1 (50)
Some or all listed as selecting materials	8 (100)	2 (40)	1 (50)
Total	8 (100)	5 (100)	2 (100)

Note: Percentages are in parentheses.

[a]Selection required (S and R).

[b]Selection prohibited (R only; neither R nor S).

[c]Selection optional (S, R, S and R; R, S and R).

their work contravene the distinction between professionals and nonprofessionals by the ALA. It is also true that libraries more oriented toward library associations are the ones that are less likely to regard library assistants as generalists. However, settings highly oriented toward library associations are as likely to view library assistants as paraprofessionals (those who may perform selection work)as they are to regard them as nonprofessionals (those who may not perform selection work). That is, paraprofessional or nonprofessional role expectations as opposed to generalist expectations tend to occur in settings collectively aware of library associations, especially in those aware of central library associations (see table 6-21). The problem does not seem to stem simply from administrative concern about reducing occupational orientations or eroding occupational control over work. These results imply that the ambiguities regarding the appropriate role of library assistants reside in the policies of the library associations and not necessarily the conditions of work in library settings.

Rather than thinking of nonprofessionals performing professional tasks as a problem, it may be more fruitful to consider the possibility that library association policies encourage organizational differentiation. In settings where work is conceptualized in terms of the abstract principles of library science, it is possible to think about library operations in abstract terms, enabling the staff to conceive of alternative ways of organizing work.[13] The ability to conceive of new forms of specialization may stretch the standards of librarianship to the limit, taking advantage of any possibility that seems credible. By providing an impetus to increase specialization, occupational institutions may run afoul of any attempt to draw hard and fast lines between professional work and the work carried out by highly qualified nonprofessionals in ancillary occupations. According to this line of reasoning, it may be impossible to avoid

Table 6-21

Role Expectations *Not* Regarding Library Assistants as Generalists as a Function of Collective Occupational Orientations

Independent Variable	Beta	Significance of Terms	R^2	Significance of Equations
Awareness of specialist associations	.297	.099	.088	.099
Awareness of central associations	.497	.004	.247	.004

Note: N = 32. No control variable. None of the organizational background or contextual variables was highly correlated with this distinction. The dependent variable was the extent to which library assistants were *not* regarded as generalists.

the problem of ambiguity in occupational role expectations. Such a problem may be endemic to all occupations and professions and may not be indicative of a lack of occupational control over work.

Conclusions

While the fit between the form of role expectations and the formality of organizational structure is undoubtedly complex, certain consistencies have emerged in the analysis. Uniformities in the form of role expectations are discernible in work settings oriented toward the same occupational point of reference—the central and specialist library associations. With other relevant factors held constant, the more aware a setting was of library associations, the more likely was specialization among librarians and among assistants to be considered acceptable. Occupational institutions appear to provide an impetus for specialization within each of these two occupations. In the case of library assistants, this impetus for specialization violated occupational norms stipulating that the selection of materials for acquisition should not be performed by non-professional staff. It may be that occupational institutions make innovative work arrangements conceivable, threatening any attempt by library associations to draw static distinctions between professional and nonprofessional work.

Occupational role expectations were unrelated to either the number or the proportion of librarians on the staff. However, the occupational composition of the support staff was relevant. The presence of library assistants and clerks was associated with generalist role expectations. Administrative responsibilities seemed to inhibit specialist role expectations for both librarians and library assistants. Size per se had no direct effect on role expectations and was not a factor giving rise to normative conceptions of an increased division of labor.

Notes

1. Impersonal rules stipulating the times and locations that certain tasks should be performed by members of a particular occupation characterize

formalized work arrangements. Participation and decision making reflect structural rather than personal considerations. People classified as having the same status attend to a similar set of roles and experience the same types of role conflicts. Given similar role sets, they take the same set of contingencies into account, face similar alternatives, and likely assess those alternatives in terms of similar priorities. Put another way, rights of participation are extended equally to those who perform the same tasks in similar circumstances. To the extent that these formalized rights are exercised or enforced as duties, the forms and rates of participation become increasingly consistent across different incumbents of the position (Dornbusch and Scott, 1975, pp. 206-207).

2. Given the small N and the need to hold constant other factors, it was necessary to employ regression analysis even though many of the measures cannot be demonstrably shown to be interval scales. A comparison of the levels of significance of Pearson's r's and Kendall's τ_b's revealed that there were no appreciable changes in the results produced by using Pearson's r. In addition to allowing several effects to be taken into account simultaneously in the same analysis, regression analysis employs statistics such as beta weights and slopes that have relatively straightforward and clear statistical and intuitive interpretations.

3. For a further discussion of statistical significance, see D.E. Morrison and R.E. Henkel, eds., *The Significance Test Controversy: A Reader* (Chicago: Aldine, 1970). The sample includes practically all (89 percent) Alberta libraries with four or more full-time positions. I do not claim, however, that this sample is statistically representative of the population of library work settings in the province, let alone those in other political jurisdictions. There is no intent to generalize my findings by the use of inferential statistics. Tests of significance are reported only as a matter of convention. Following Zelditch (1962), I suggest that it is my theory and not my results that may be generalized.

4. In small samples like this one ($N = 32$), we can discern only very large correlations. In larger samples such as national opinion polls, much smaller effects can be differentiated with some confidence from chance.

5. In six cases the library setting was a department in a larger library. In the case of these larger libraries, their characteristics are not represented by the departmental work settings included in the sample.

6. This study focuses specifically on the technical level of organization (Parsons, 1960) where work is carried out in libraries. Organizational theory and empirical studies have tended to center on the managerial level of organization, presuming that the structure of the bureaucratic or administrative component of an organization would be reflected in the structure of work settings at the technical level of operation. The results of this study question this assumption.

7. Before I conducted the survey, it had seemed possible for some organizations to perform the same functions as associations representing an occupation. For instance, certain hospitals are well known for developing new medical procedures and new knowledge. These hospitals exercise control over less specialized and prestigious hospitals through a process of defining medical

technology and medical ethics. Because this possibility was not well understood, a measure to distinguish among organizations was not developed in advance of this analysis. This distinction, however, does seem to account for some of the differences between these four libraries and the twenty-eight others.

8. The validity of creating a variable that ordered the three types of library settings along a central-peripheral dimension was confirmed by the use of dummy variables in the regression analyses. An examination of the slope coefficients of the two dummy variables representing the cut-points on the three-point scale showed that the relationships with the dependent variables on tables 6-10 and 7-4 were monotonic and not appreciably curvilinear. Generally, the introduction of the two dummy variables in the place of the single type-of-library variable did not alter the overall pattern of results (that is, the slope and beta coefficients) in any of the regression analyses reported in this book.

9. Berger and Luckman (1966, pp. 67-72) argue that it is this reflexive character of socialization by teaching that makes social reality appear to be objectively real to both the teacher and the learner.

10. Price (1972, p. 174) defines size as "the scale of operations of a social system. In an organization, . . . the scale of operations is indicated by such observables as the number of personnel, the amount of assets, and the degree of expenditures."

11. Although it was possible to demonstrate that behavior tended to conform to role expectations, it proved to be impossible to study the pattern of behavior instead of the pattern of expectations. Detailed descriptions of behavior were available only for those occupational statuses that were performing reference and selection in the "last week"—the week prior to the administration of the questionnaire in the setting. The survey was conducted during the summer months, a slack period for most libraries and the time when many personnel took holidays. In addition, data on the behavior of any particular occupation were available for only a subset of the cases. Generally, the results for one occupation could not be compared with those for another. Each occupation was found in a different subset of the cases. More important, interaction effects were present in the data. The same factors tended to behave differently in different subsets of the cases. Given the reduced number of cases, it was all but impossible to redress this problem.

12. Meyer and Rowan comment on this possibility in an article entitled, "Formal Structure of Organizations as Myth and Ceremony." "As rationalizing institutional myths arise in existing domains of activities, extant organizations expand their formal structures so as to become isomorphic with these new myths" (1977, p. 345).

13. See Stinchcombe (1965, pp. 150-151) on general literacy and specialized schooling and Scott (1970 pp. 313-315) on formalization and rationality.

7

The Pattern of Communication

If work arrangements reflect institutions of librarianship, communication should tend to flow from those who select materials for acquisition toward those who provide reference service. The form of interaction linking one task to another reflects the technology employed in a work setting. Thompson (1967), among others, distinguished between technologies that are conceived to consist of sequential interdependence and those that involve feedback. The pattern of communication may indicate the presence of one type of contingency or the other. Communication may be initiated in one direction only, linking one task to another serially or initiated in both directions in reciprocal fashion. According to the policies of representative library associations, selection seems conceived to be causally prior to reference in library operations.

In part, librarians who select materials are expected to take the initiative in gathering information about the needs of library users. In addition, librarians are directed to guide the work of nonlibrarians. Librarians are expected to supervise reference services provided by nonlibrarians. The principles and standards of librarianship as articulated by library associations provide a blueprint of appropriate modes of library operation, including appropriate patterns of communication. It would be predicted that communication initiated by those who select materials (librarians in most cases) would be more likely to occur in settings collectively oriented toward the librarian occupation. When the distinction between noninnovative and innovative libraries is taken into account, the data are consistent with this prediction.

Variations from One Library to Another

Every possible pattern of communication between selection and reference activities was found among the thirty-two cases sampled. Of particular interest were patterns that included contacts initiated by those who selected materials for acquisition, since librarians were typically the ones who selected materials. Table 7-1 shows the incidence of each type of interaction. In 37 percent of the settings, the composite pattern of communication included interaction initiated only by those who selected materials. (In those settings, some or all of those who provided reference service did not initiate interaction in return.) In another 22 percent of the cases, communication from selection to reference existed in reciprocal form only. (Those who provided reference service also

Table 7-1

The Initiation of Communication between Those Who Select Materials for Acquisition and Those Who Provide Reference Service

Interaction	Frequency	Percentage
High: Communication initiated from selection to reference (four possible composite patterns)	12	37
$S \rightarrow R$, plus $S \rightleftharpoons R^a$	5	
$S \rightarrow R$, plus $S \rightleftharpoons R$ and $R \rightarrow S$	3	
$S \rightarrow R$, plus $R \rightarrow S$	2	
$S \rightarrow R$ only[b]	2	
Moderate: Communication initiated from selection to reference reciprocated (two possible composite patterns)	7	22
$S \rightleftharpoons R$, plus $R \rightarrow S$	6	
$S \rightleftharpoons R$ only[c]	1	
Low: No communication from selection to reference (two possible patterns)	13	41
$R \rightarrow S$ only[d]	8	
No communication	5	

[a]$S \rightarrow R$, plus $S \rightleftharpoons R$: Communication initiated only by those who select materials between some pairs of individuals, plus communication reciprocated between other pairs of individuals.

[b]$S \rightarrow R$ only: Communication initiated only by those who select materials.

[c]$S \rightleftharpoons R$ only: Communication between those who select materials and those who provide reference always reciprocated.

[d]$R \rightarrow S$ only: Communication initiated only by those who provide reference service.

initiated interaction in return toward those who selected materials.) Thus in 59 percent of the sample the pattern of communication corresponded more or less with the institutions of librarianship as outlined by library associations (The pattern of communication was scored as either high or moderate.) However, in 41 percent of the cases, the pattern of communication did not correspond at all to those precepts (the pattern of communication was scored as low).

Authoritative Communication

The occupational institutions aritculated by those associations imply the following.

1. Selection ought to be performed by librarians only. (Clerks ought to be expected to perform reference but not selection,)

2. Librarians ought to set policy with regard to selection and reference,
3. Librarians ought to personally supervise and regulate all selection and reference work carried out by others,
4. In public libraries librarians ought to consult those in contact with library users (those who perform reference tasks) to obtain information relevant to the selection of materials.

If librarians discharged their duties in accordance with these canons, the composite pattern of interaction would include communication initiated by those who select materials for acquisition. Given the authority differential separating librarians and nonlibrarians, these contacts could also include communicating instructions or other unsolicited advice as well as keeping in touch with reference work carried out by others.

The policies of library associations do not elaborate on communication flowing from those who perform reference services (nonlibrarians as well as librarians) to those who select materials (usually librarians). Interaction initiated by those who carry out reference tasks probably involved informal consultation. By keeping in touch with those who had selected the materials, those who provided reference service could keep informed about current library holdings. Because selection tasks tended to be performed by those with authority, communication initiated by those who provided reference service often flowed upward from subordinate to superior. A clerk would contact a librarian in order to seek advice, to request assistance, or to pass on the more involved requests for reference assistance. In most libraries clerks were expected to screen the requests of library users, handling the simpler jobs themselves and referring the rest to a librarian.

Where communication flowed only from those who carried out reference to those who performed selection (where there is no communication from selection to reference), those in authority would be in a position of passively receiving contacts initiated by their subordinates. Rather than giving instructions or orders and taking the initiative to check on work done, those in charge would respond only to problems identified by their subordinates. They would provide assistance only on request. This extreme state of affairs would violate standards set by central library associations.

The data in table 7-2 are consistent with the interpretation that contacts initiated from those who performed selection to those carrying out reference involve some form of authoritative communication. Communication from selection to reference tended to occur when clerks were expected to perform reference tasks only. The results are most pronounced when one looks at the settings in which contacts are initiated only by those who select material (64 percent versus 27 percent). If clerks as well as librarians carried out both reference and selection, the coordination of these two activities could be accomplished largely by individuals[1] organizing their own work. Restricting clerks

Table 7-2

The Patterns of Communication Associated with Role Expectations Limiting
Library Clerks to Performing Reference Work Only
(*percent*)

	Role Expectations for Library Clerks	
Pattern	Reference Only	Other Alternatives Involving Selection
No communication from selection to reference	18 (2)	37 (4)
Selection to reference in reciprocal $(S \rightleftharpoons R)$	18 (2)	36 (4)
From selection to reference only $(S \rightarrow R)$	64 (7)	27 (3)
Total	100 (11)	100 (11)

Note: Frequencies are in parentheses. Five settings in which no communication was reported to exist were excluded in addition to seven settings in which library clerks were expected to perform neither reference nor selection. Two settings were excluded on both grounds.

to performing only reference work would create a "need" for librarians to supervise library clerks. With this division of labor, supervision by those in authority would become one of the primary mechanisms in addition to formal regulation for coordinating selection and reference work within library settings.

Information-Gathering Communication

Contact initiated by those who select materials could also be indicative of an information-gathering process. Procedures outlined by the ALA and echoed by other central associations encourage librarians to assess the needs of library clientele in the course of selecting materials for their use. In educational or special libraries, where many if not most users are specialists or professionals in their own right, librarians are directed to contact the clients themselves. However, for public libraries, the policy is that librarians should contact staff members in touch with library users, in addition to any consultation with library patrons. The results in table 7-3 correspond to these policies. Communication in which contact is initiated only by those who select materials is found most frequently in public libraries (67 percent) as opposed to educational (50 percent) and business or government libraries (13 percent). (In fully 50 percent of the business and government libraries, no communication is initiated

Table 7-3
The Pattern of Communication by Type of Library
(*percent*)

	Type of Library		
Pattern	*Public*	*Educational*	*Business or Government*
No communication from selection to reference	11 (1)	30 (3)	50 (4)
Selection to reference in reciprocal form only (S ⇌ R)	22 (2)	20 (2)	37 (3)
Selection to reference only (S → R)	67 (6)	50 (5)	13 (1)
Total	100 (9)	100 (10)	100 (8)

Note: Frequencies are in parentheses. Five settings that reported no communication were excluded.

by those who select materials.) Whether initiative exercised by those who select materials involves consultation or supervision, both forms of communication would have the effect of coordinating selection and reference work in the setting.

Occupational Orientations and Type of Library

The results in tables 7-2 and 7-3 show that it may be possible to interpret the pattern of communication in terms of occupational institutions. The occupational orientation of a setting would be indicative of the relevance of occupational institutions to current work arrangements. The greater the relevance of occupational institutions in the setting, the greater the possibility that interaction would be initiated by those who select materials for acquisition. This hypothesis is consistent with the data reported in table 7-4 and summarized in figure 7-1.

Communication initiated by those who select materials for acquisition tends to occur in library settings oriented toward the librarian occupation and in public libraries as opposed to business or government libraries. The distinction between innovative and the more conventional libraries is of importance. Although innovative libraries are quite aware of library associations, the pattern of communication in such work settings approximates that in libraries that are not oriented toward the librarian occupation. Just as they avoided any vestiges

Table 7-4

The Pattern of Communication as a Function of Collective Occupational Orientations

Independent Variables	Beta	Significance of Terms	R^2	Significance of Equations
Awareness of specialist associations[a]	.411	.041	.344	.007
Type of library	.259	.130		
Number of professional librarians	.045	.804		
Awareness of central associations[a]	.452	.008	.410	.002
Type of library	.259	.103		
Number of professional librarians	.131	.397		
Coincidence of values and interests[a]	.267	.127	.299	.018
Type of library	.326	.058		
Number of professional librarians	.169	.320		

Note: $N = 32$. The control variables were the threshold of professional librarians and the type of library. The dependent variable was communication from selection to reference. See Reeves (1978, p. 257) for a correlation matrix of the independent, control, and dependent variables.

[a]Ranking innovative libraries as completely unoriented toward the occupation.

of formal regulation, job descriptions, or written records, innovative libraries also seemed to avoid any hint of a centralized pattern of communication.

The effect of the number of librarians on the pattern of communication is almost entirely mediated by the occupational orientation of the setting. Without an orientation toward the occupation, an orientation shared by non-librarians and librarians alike, the presence of two or more librarians appears to have little direct effect on the pattern of interaction between selection and reference. It seems reasonable to presume that the presence of several librarians contributes to the occupational orientation of others in the setting. In turn, the occupational orientation of the setting facilitates conformity with the standards set by the representative associations. In this way the internal patterns of communication could be modeled on occupational standards set by library associations. Occupational institutions would provide an aura of legitimacy for contacts initiated by those who select materials for acquisition.

This argument holds only for noninnovative library settings. It is in those settings, and not the four innovative settings, that communication initiated by those who select materials is correlated with a collective occupational orientation. If the four innovative settings were excluded from the analysis, the correlation between the indicators of occupational orientation and the threshold number of librarians would increase in magnitude, increasing the extent to which

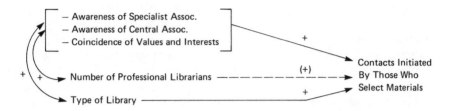

Collective Occupational
Orientations[a]

— Awareness of Specialist Assoc.
— Awareness of Central Assoc.
— Coincidence of Values and Interests

+

Contacts Initiated
By Those Who
Select Materials

(+)

+   +   Number of Professional Librarians — — — — — — — —(+)— — —

+

Type of Library

[a]Ranking innovative libraries as completely unoriented toward the occupation.

Figure 7-1. Pattern of Communication as a Function of Collective Occupational Orientations and the Type of Library

occupational orientation mediates the statistical relationship between the number of librarians and the pattern of communication.

The relationship between the pattern of communication and the type of library might be interpreted in terms of association policies on consultation vis-à-vis the selection of materials. If this interpretation has merit, holding the type of library statistically constant should reduce the magnitude of the association between occupational orientation and the pattern of consultation. Only part of the effect of the correlation between the type of library and communication may be a product of occupational orientations. In this event holding the level of occupational orientations statistically constant would reduce to zero the direct effect of library type on communication. The correlation was, in fact, only partially reduced (the correlation was initially 0.43, while beta = 0.259, 0.259, or 0.326, for the three regression analyses). If the four innovative settings were excluded from the analysis, the correlation between the indicators of occupational orientation and the type of library increases. As a consequence, simultaneously entering the type of library and collective occupational orientations into the regression analysis would reduce the direct effect of each factor on the pattern of communication. However, the type of library continues to have an independent effect on communication over and above the qualifications in library association policies prescribing different patterns of communication in different types of libraries.

The flow of communication is more likely to be centralized in the hands of the librarians in public libraries and least likely to be centralized in business or government libraries. Business and government libraries are integral parts of larger, nonlibrary organizations. They are highly dependent on the larger organization for both needed resources and continued demand for their services. Library policies reflect the goals of the business or the government department rather than the priorities of the library as a library. Business and government departments regulate demand for library services much in the same way that it regulates the use of other support services. Those who use the library on a regular basis are typically officials, professionals, or technical experts whose organizational authority, power, and status as well as technical knowledge of subject matter often exceed those of the librarian. Ancillary staff generally work for a number of bosses—a number of important library users in addition to the librarian. The result is that library staff, including the librarian in charge, defer to the wishes of important patrons. These patrons, not the librarian, take the initiative in directing and organizing the reference work performed by library staff. The impact on the pattern of communication is clear. If communication occurs at all, those providing reference take the initiative. Communication is rarely initiated by those who are selecting materials for acquisition (the flow of communication   prescribed by library associations). Librarians lose their capacity to supervise the work of others and to monopolize information on the current state of library operations. The autonomy of the librarian to personally direct and organize reference work tends to be compromised in business and government libraries. To a much lesser extent librarians in university and college libraries may also experience some loss of autonomy for similar reasons. Librarians in public libraries are least likely to have their autonomy threatened from this quarter. The loss of autonomy poses a direct threat to the librarians's occupational authority and control over library work.

Conclusions

The data revealed that library settings oriented toward the same occupational point of reference tend to possess similar work arrangements. In accordance with occupational standards, librarians tended to take the initiative in consulting and supervising others who carried out reference work. This was especially true where clerks were restricted to providing reference service and where library patrons tended to be nonexperts (in public libraries). The number of librarians on the staff may have an indirect effect on the pattern of interaction by increasing collective awareness of library associations. Neither the size nor the complexity of the library setting was correlated with the pattern of communication. However, the type of library had an independent effect on communication. The autonomy and occupational authority of the librarian appear to be compromised in business and government libraries and, to a lesser extent, in university and college libraries.

8

The Status
of the Librarian

In every library surveyed, librarians had more authority and were considered to have more personal status than any nonlibrarians. Similarly, library clerks were consistently accorded the least authority and the least interpersonal influence. This power and authority structure was invariant across all settings. The problem is not that of identifying the conditions under which librarians possess authority on the job—they possess authority in all work settings. Rather, the problem is to identify the conditions under which librarians were more likely to derive their authority from their occupational status rather than from their managerial position. The correlation between work arrangements that correspond to library association policies and collective occupational orientations suggests the answer to this problem.

Librarians are more likely to derive their authority from their occupational status in occupationally oriented settings. In those settings librarians are more likely to establish a formal system of job descriptions and written records in accordance with occupational standards. Librarians, as the persons who do most of the selection of materials for acquisition, tend to take the initiative in their dealings with other, supervising the work of those providing reference service and collective information on the state of library operations. In short, it is in occupationally oriented settings that librarians are more likely to institute a system of library administration that conforms to occupational norms. This system of administration gives the librarian the initiative in planning work arrangements, schedules, and systems of records. This system of administration also concentrates the flow of information in the hands of the librarian. Not only is the authority of the librarian interpreted, explained, and justified in terms of occupational institutions, but the system of administration puts the librarian in a position that reaffirms the existence of those institutions.

According to library association policies, libraries are charged with the responsibility for the administration of library services: "stipulating job descriptions," "establishing regulations and guidelines," "supervising . . . assigned work," and "developing a system of required records and statistics" among other duties. Our analysis of the results of the survey of library settings revealed considerable variations from one library to another in the structure of work arrangements, positive correlations between collective occupational orientations and work arrangements that conform to the standards stipulated in library association policies, and no consistent correlation between these work arrangements and the organizational characteristics of the libraries. When other relevant factors were statistically held constant, occupationally oriented work settings were more likely to have job descriptions, written records, and consensus on role expectations; they were more likely to display appropriate patterns of supervision and information gathering; and they were more likely to entertain the possibility of specialization. The results of the regression analyses on which these generalizations are based appear in table 8-1.

Occupational Factors

Library Associations

The collective awareness of library associations was the most consistent indicator of occupational orientations. In comparison, the measures of orientation toward librarians as an occupational group—"interest in professional librarians" and "the coincidence of values and interests" between the library and the occupation— were correlated with only a few of the measures of organizational structure. These results emphasize the important role that library associations play within the occupation. Whether or not most practicing librarians are active members, these associations establish the librarian's claim of competence, define the task domain of the librarians, and articulate the standards of library service that place the librarian in charge of library operations. In the absence of representative associations or schools, it seems unlikely that the occupation would have an impact on conditions of work in any library.

Collective Occupational Orientations

In addition to underlining the importance of library associations, the survey also gave us some idea of the significance of collective occupational orientations to occupational authority. The survey revealed that the librarian's orientations reflected the collective orientations of others in the setting, but that the librarian's comprehension of relevant library association policies was vague and nonspecific. In chapter 4 we found that the librarian's individual level of awareness of library associations was more closely attuned to the level of awareness of nonlibrarians on their staff than to the awareness of librarians as an occupational group outside the library. Awareness tended to be similar within each setting and to vary between settings. Thus librarians in different settings had different levels of personal awareness even though they were members of the same occupation and were all graduates of accredited schools of library science. When questioned about their familiarity with standards prescribed by library associations, most librarians reported only a general knowledge of these issues

Table 8-1
A Summary of the Results of the Regression Analyses

Dependent Variables: Structure of Work Arrangements	Occupational Orientations					Organizational Properties				
	Associations		Librarians as a Group				Size		Composition	
	Central	Specialist	Interest	Coincidence	Type	Circulation	Budget	Positions	LA	LC
Centralized communication (S → R)	+	+		+	+					
Formalization										
Job descriptions										
Reference	+	+	+	+		−				
Selection	+	+		+		−				
Written records										
Reference	+	+					+			
Selection	+	+								
Role expectations										
Consensus[a]										
Library clerks	+	+	+							
Library assistants		+	+					−		
Specialist latitude										
Professional librarian	+	+							−	
Library assistants	+	+							−	
Library assistants										
Not generalists	+									−

[a]For all correlations except those regarding consensus, the measures of occupational orientations ranked innovative libraries as completely unoriented toward the occupation.

and policies. The vast majority of the librarians were not members of these associations and did not attend their meetings on a regular basis. Many kept track of some issues and policies in their discussions with others or by reading newsletters or journals. (Librarians in so few libraries engaged in any one activity on a regular basis that it was impossible to create variables measuring those behaviors.) When asked whether the actual practices of their particular library parallelled the ideals of those associations whose issues and policies they kept track of, only a handful felt that any parallels existed, and when pressed for details, they were unable to articulate their impressions with any degree of specificity. Rather than measuring an internalized set of standards or comprehensive base of knowledge, occupational orientations for librarians seemed to represent a propensity to gain a detailed knowledge of occupational standards on an "as needed" basis. Like a doctor who studies in preparation for a new operation, occupationally oriented librarians are prepared to consult others in the occupation and to research the library journals and the policies of library associations when altering existing work arrangements.

A librarian's status on the job did not appear to be a product of personal knowledge of current standards outlined in the policies of library associations. Rather, the librarian's status was derived from social circumstances—the normative foundations of the occupation and the orientations of others, including nonlibrarians, with whom the librarian worked. A high level of collective occupational orientation among the library staff was indicative of a willingness to acknowledge the librarian's superior status and a readiness to accept work arrangements justified in terms of occupational standards. In the absence of these social circumstances, librarians appeared to accommodate their personal orientations and their library's system of operation to local norms. In the presence of these social circumstances, librarians enhanced their status and authority by instituting a system of library service in accordance with occupational norms.

Innovative Libraries

A third strand in the occupational organization of libraries seems to be manifested in the distinction between innovative and more conventional library settings. Innovative libraries were leading organizations in the region. They had attracted the services of highly "professional" librarians who succeeded in acquainting nonlibrarians on the staff with central and specialist library associations. Still, innovative libraries went out of their way to avoid using job descriptions and written records. Occupational role expectations in these libraries did not give latitude for specialization, tending to require librarians (but not library assistants) to be generalists. In addition, the initiative in the pattern of communication did not lie with those who selected materials. Rather, it resided with those who provided reference service. An impression gained during the interviews was that librarians felt that the standardized procedures for library administration as proposed in the official policies of central library associations were not appropriate for their unique circumstances and purposes. Rejection of the more obvious trappings of formal regulation and supervision (but not consensus on role expectations) seemed to be a natural consequence of this sentiment.

Organizational Factors

The Presence of Librarians

Librarians are more likely to enjoy this professional status in settings employing greater numbers of librarians and with larger acquisition's budgets. (See appendix B for a discussion of organizational factors that were *not* related to occupational work arrangements.) Because librarians constitute the dominant occupation, their presence on the staff affects the collective orientations of others: the greater their numbers, the higher the level of collective orientations toward library associations. The relevance of the occupation as a reference group varies in direct proportion to the numbers of librarians on staff. Thus the mere presence of two or more librarians enhances the occupational authority of the librarian. If the presence of librarians has any effect on the structure of work arrangements, it does so by influencing collective orientations. We found that positive correlations with occupational work arrangements were reduced when occupational orientations were statistically held constant. See figure 8-1.

The Size of the Acquisitions Budget

The extent of outside funding received by a library also seems to affect the orientations of the staff. The larger the acquisitions budget, the greater the collective awareness of library associations. It seems that libraries must provide some rationale to obtain and sustain high levels of financial support. Library associations (and schools) provide standards of operation and accounting procedures that enable the staff to justify and explain their budgets. The expertise and hence the authority of the librarian are highlighted in libraries with larger budgets. In addition, librarians in libraries with larger budgets are more likely to institute a system of records, reinforcing their authority in the work setting. Of course, libraries with larger budgets are the ones with greater numbers of librarians on the staff. In practice, these two factors frequently combine to emphasize the occupational status of the librarian.

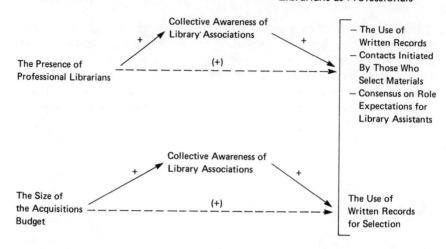

Figure 8-1. The Collective Awareness of Library Associations Mediates the
Effect of the Presence of Professional Librarians and the Size
of the Acquisitions Budget on Some Library Work Arrangements

The Size of Library Operations

The occupational status of the librarian and the capacity to institute the proper
system of library administration are impaired under certain conditions. The
combination of a large circulation with a large staff probably interferes with
attempts to establish a formal system of control in accordance with occupational norms. Job descriptions in libraries with larger circulations tend to be
eroded by a process of debureaucratization. Library users are often unfamiliar
with the formal rules and regulations of the library. In those libraries with a
high volume of transactions between the staff and clients, the staff tends to
accommodate clients at the expense of formal organizational procedures (see
figure 6-3). In addition, these libraries tend to have larger numbers of personnel. As a result, consensus among the staff on the appropriate duties and
responsibilities for library clerks is also reduced (see figure 6-1). The sheer
size of the library's operations limited the librarian's ability to design and
plan work arrangements.

Type of Library

The type of library has a bearing on the status of the librarian. The autonomy
of the librarian to personally supervise and direct the work of library staff
is reduced in business and government libraries and, to some extent, in university

and college libraries. Several factors combine to threaten the central position of the librarian: (1) the dependence on an encompassing, nonlibrary organization for finances and demand for library services; (2) the capacity of the encompassing organization to subject the library, as one of several service departments, to general operating procedures, and (3) the tendency of library staff to defer to the superior organizational authority or technical expertise of library users. Under these conditions the support staff tend to do reference work under the direction of important library users rather than under the direction of the librarian (see figure 7-1).

There is a literature that claims that there is an inherent difference between professional and administrative authority. The threat of bureaucratic restriction on the autonomy of professionals who work in organizations is regarded as a source of tension and conflict (Parsons, 1947, pp. 59-60; Etzioni, 1964, pp. 75-93; Scott, 1966). The correlation between type of library and occupational orientations suggests why this tension and conflict was not apparent in our sample of libraries. This threat to professional autonomy was greatest in business and government libraries, those settings least likely to be occupationally oriented. It was in precisely those settings that librarians were not likely to enjoy an occupational source of authority (where occupational orientations are low) that the threat existed. Lacking a staff that endorsed occupational standards or indicated a willingness to voluntarily comply with the exercise of occupational authority, librarians are unlikely to challenge these threats to their right to establish an occupational system of library administration. In the absence of collective support in the work setting, conflict would not be expected to erupt between an individual inner-directed librarian and bureaucrats in the larger organization. Indeed, given low levels of collective occupational orientations, the librarian may not even be attuned to the occupational model for library operations. (Recall that the librarian's personal level of awareness was aligned more with the awareness of their co-workers in the setting than with the awareness of other librarians in other settings.) Conditions favored the existence of an occupational base of authority in public libraries, but the threat in library operations of outside interference is lowest in this type of library. Again, conflict or tension fails to emerge because the conditions that engender occupational authority do not tend to coexist with this threat. For conflict or tension to be apparent, the correlation between occupational orientations and library type would have had to be negative rather than positive.

We must remind ourselves again that occupational orientations and type of library have statistically independent effects on communication in library settings. Although these two processes work simultaneously, they have independent effects on the pattern of communication. This was demonstrated in figure 7-1 and table 7-4. Thus librarians in business and government libraries lack authority and control, in part because of the low level of occupational orientation and in part because of the organizational threat to their autonomy. The informed observer who did not use statistical procedures to identify the independent effect of occupational orientations and the type of library might spuriously attribute the combined effect to the threat to occupational autonomy and ignore the effect of collective occupational orientations or, conversely, spuriously attribute the combined effect to occupational orientations and ignore the effect of the type of library. In the literature on professionalism, the former has been the typical response. The significance of collective occupational orientations to occupational authority and control over library work arrangements is lost. The emphasis on threats to occupational autonomy in the professionalism literature has blinded us to sources of occupational authority that are available to members of "nonprofessional" occupations.

Amending the Conventional Interpretation

The conventional conception of professional authority lies at the heart of this misunderstanding. The typical argument for explaining why librarians are not professionals is that librarians and other semiprofessionals, technocrats, and technicians are not considered to be professionals because they lack autonomy in organizational work settings. Professionals are characterized by their commitment to service to clients—service in accordance with the principles and standards of the profession, not necessarily with the needs perceived by clients or other nonprofessionals. Thus it is not enough to be committed to providing service; the practitioner must have the professional authority to render service in accordance with the norms of the profession. Because of this requirement, it is claimed that the librarian occupation lacks a service commitment. Certainly, library associations and schools give primacy to providing library service as an occupational objective. However, for a variety of reasons, librarians are not thought to possess the professional authority necessary to honor that commitment. It is presumed that professional authority is derived from mastery of an esoteric body of knowledge, vested rights to prescribe and enforce standards of practice, and the power to limit competition— the attributes of a powerful profession. Because librarians belong to a weak occupation, they must rely on their administrative position in the organization rather than their occupational status for authority. This accommodation subverts occupational control over library service and is regarded as a major impediment to the eventual attainment of professional status (Goode, 1961; North, 1976).

This conventional interpretation of the librarian's status is correct when it predicts that threats to occupational autonomy weaken the librarian's control over library service. In business and government libraries, reference work provided by the library staff tends to be supervised by important library users—executives, professionals, technicians—rather than by the librarian. Rather than taking the initiative in defining how reference service is to be provided, the librarian tends to passively respond to problems identified by their subordinates and by library users.

This conventional interpretation is probably correct in assuming that librarians would be more capable of resisting such threats if their occupation possessed the structural powers of an established profession. If library associations and schools had such powers, the management business and government organizations could enforce procedures that ran counter to occupational standards only at the risk of inviting, in reprisal, collective action from the occupation or legal prosecution by the occupation or the state.

However, this conventional interpretation is incorrect when it presumes that occupational authority is based on the structural power of the occupation to enforce standards. If this were correct, it would be impossible to find any correlation between the standards of library service espoused by library associations and actual library practices. Nevertheless, when the type of library (the threat to occupational autonomy) was statistically held constant, the correlation between standards of library service and actual library practices increased as the level of collective occupational orientation increased. Indeed, this finding endures when every other relevant organizational factor is entered into the analysis and held constant. In order to explain these findings we must amend our explanation for occupational authority. Occupational authority is established by the conjunction of a well-defined task domain outside the work setting and collective occupational orientations within the setting. The structural power of profession contributes to the authority of practitioners by increasing occupational orientations in work settings. As such, structural power is only a sufficient condition for achieving high levels of occupational orientation; it is not a necessary condition for occupational authority and control over work.

The conventional interpretation of the librarian's status is also incorrect when it presumes that bureaucratic mechanisms of control are antithetical to occupational authority. Far from being alien to the ideals of library service and librarianship, job descriptions, written records, and a centralized pattern of communication are prescribed elements of the appropriate system of library administration. In occupationally oriented settings, occupational control over work arrangements tends to produce an administrative position for the librarian, providing organizational structures that can be used to enforce occupational standards and reinforce occupational authority. The occupation, not the organization, promotes bureaucratic control in library work settings.

Part III
The Impact of the Library on
Occupational Orientations and
Work Arrangements

9

The Occupation, Not the Organization, Promotes Bureaucratic Control within Library Work Settings

It has been generally accepted that professionalization and bureaucratization should be negatively correlated. Scott (1965, pp. 267-268) regarded professional and bureaucratic models of organizing work as alternatives to one another. "Professionals are . . . equipped with internalized control mechanisms and bureaucrats are usually thought of as . . . operating in a hierarchical structure under a system of formal rules" (p. 268). Because professionals possess technical expertise and have internalized relevant rules of conduct, formal regulation of their work is deemed to be not necessary. In a study that employed several measures of each concept Hall (1968) confirmed that professionalism and bureaucratization were inversely related. He "hypothesized that the more developed the normative system of the occupations in an organization, the less need for a highly bureaucratized organizational system" (p. 101). Both the results of this study and their interpretation appear to be fundamentally at odds with the literature.

A change in the unit of analysis may account for these differences. In quantitative, survey research, professionalism typically refers to personal attitudes or orientations of individual practitioners (Goldberg, 1976), the percentage of professionals in the organization with professional orientations (Hall, 1968), the percentage of employees in the organization possessing certain educational qualifications (Blau, 1968; Blau, Heydebrand, and Stauffer, 1966), or the structural foundations of the occupation itself (Hall, 1968; Hickson and Thomas, 1969). Bureaucratization may refer to personal perceptions of the individual's lack of autonomy and control (Goldberg, 1976), the proportion of managers in the organization (Blau, 1968; Blau, Heydebrand, and Stauffer, 1966), or the structural characteristics of organization's system of management (Udy, 1959; Hall, 1968; Aiken and Hage, 1969; Inkson, Pugh, and Hickson, 1970). Our interpretation of the data depends on whether the indicators represent the personal properties of the individual respondent or global characteristics of the organization and whether the correlation is calculated using the individual or the organization as the unit of analysis (Pennings, 1974). Hall's results are most relevant for this study. According to our data, we would tend to expect personal occupational orientations to approximate collective occupational orientations in the work setting. Hall found that the proportion of professionals in an organization that personally "used the professional organization as a major reference was negatively correlated with all indicators of bureaucratization in the organization as a whole. "The subjects in each organization responded to the items according to the degree to which the statement corresponded to their own conception of the organization" (Hall, 1958, p. 96). In particular, the proportion was negatively correlated with "organizationally developed techniques of dealing with work settings" (1968, p. 102). If "organizationally developed techniques of dealing with work settings" refers to procedures created by management outside the work setting and not to standardized work arrangements inspired by occupational institutions, no contradiction exists between Hall's results and those reported in this study. Hall's findings would be consistent with a hypothesis that occupationally based authority structures within the work setting and bureaucratic structures of authority at the managerial level outside the work setting are alternative forms of control. It is possible that most analyses of survey data correlate personal professionalism with managerially centered bureaucratization. None of the survey studies reported in the literature saw a need to clearly distinguish between standardization within the work setting and managerial bureaucratization, undoubtably presuming that the former is solely a function of the latter.

No simple relationship exists between standardization in the work setting and bureaucratization at the managerial level. We found that the association between regulation acknowledged in the work setting and official documentation and recordkeeping was rather low. Collective occupational orientations were correlated with standardization of work arrangements in the work setting, not with official documentation and recordkeeping at the managerial level. The controlling character of occupationally based authority in the work setting is not derived from enforcement from outside the setting, either from management or from occupational associations. Thus empirically and theoretically, standardization in the work setting and managerial-level bureaucratization are seen as independent phenomena.

This is not to suggest that collective occupational orientations within the setting are unaffected by the organizational administration outside the setting. For instance, the threat of bureaucratic intervention, sanctioning work arrangements that conform to managerial standards and priorities, may either attenuate or reinforce occupational orientations, again indirectly affecting occupational work arrangements in the setting. Members of an occupation and bureaucrats need not necessarily conflict with one another. Senior administrators may endorse occupational standards and procedures, considering this course of action to be more efficient and effective than exercising management's prerogative to design organizational work flows and authority structures. Members of an occupation may accede to managerial assignments and objectives if they support the occupational dominance order. Should it occur, conflict would be predicted to exist between two collectivities—between those in a professionally oriented work setting and those in a managerially oriented work setting. (In the absence of collective support conflict would not be expected to occur between an individual, inner-directed professional and the bureaucratic system.) Without knowledge of the actions of management vis-à-vis the occupation, it would be impossible to predict the direction of the correlation between occupational orientations within the work setting and the extent of bureaucratization outside the work setting. This correlation could conceivably be either positive or negative.

We are still left with the fact that this study contradicts the popular notion that professionals, if left to their own devices, work in informally organized settings. This idea rests on the argument that because professionals can institute their own system of control over work in the setting, they do not require bureaucratic coordination by management (at least not within the work setting), and their work in the setting is therefore organized on an informal basis. Assuming that management is the sole source of standardization of work, the absence of bureaucratic control by management is equated with informal work arrangements. Making this same assumption, the negative correlation between personal occupational orientations and organizational bureaucratization is thought to confirm the idea that the authority and control exercised by professionals is informal in nature. The assumption on which both the interpretation of survey results and the argument rests is open to question. We cannot infer the degree of formality or informality of occupational authority and control from knowledge of the extent of managerially centered bureaucratization in the organization as a whole. In order to assess the formality of occupational authority and control in organizational work settings, we must investigate the correlation between occupational orientations and standardization at the level of the work setting itself. This survey was specifically designed to do just that. The finding that occupational orientations and standardization are positively correlated in library settings agrees with Eliot Friedson's (1970) observations that the professional dominance hierarchy in hospital settings is formally organized. Contrary to Scott's (1965) distinction between professional and bureaucratic models of organization, Friedson suggests that the position of authority held by the physician bears a close resemblance to a position of authority in a bureaucracy. In the last section of this book a theory of occupational authority is developed that accounts for the parallels between Friedson's analysis of the medical professions and this study of the librarian occupation.

Occupational Processes

Bureaucracy refers to centralization of authority in the hands of a specialized administrative staff who regulate and coordinate the activities of participants by standardizing and planning a system of organization (Scott, 1970, p. 318). The policies of library associations advocate routine control procedures but not necessarily the existence of a distinct staff that performs only administrative tasks. Librarians are enjoined to create a system of library administration that centralizes authority in the hands of the librarian. Librarians are expected to regulate and coordinate the activities of the library's staff and users. They are to do this by instituting guidelines, job descriptions, and systems of record-keeping as well as by maintaining personal supervision over library work. Thus in theory at least, librarians ought to employ bureaucratic procedures of library administration.

In practice occupational control does seem to be associated with bureau-cratic administrative procedures. Job descriptions, written records, and a pattern of communication consistent with professional supervision and information-gathering tended to exist in the more occupationally oriented library settings. If these processes favoring occupational control and authority were the only ones affecting library organization (that is, if no other, nonoccupational process was relevant), occupationally oriented libraries would possess a coherent system of bureaucratic control. Job descriptions and written records are of particular interest because they should be integral components of an organization's internal system of formal control. Job descriptions allocate responsibilities in the per-formance of specific tasks to incumbents of particular positions. They also specify basic standards and suggest criteria by which performance is evaluated. Written records as well as the patterns of supervision and information gathering would provide information about the accomplishment of specified tasks. By combining a system of task descriptions with a system of recordkeeping, the formal control apparatus should become more coherent and presumably, more effective (Scott, Dornbusch, Bushing, and Laing, 1967).

The importance of administration to the librarian occupation has not escaped notice. Goode (1961, pp. 314-315), Knapp (1973, pp. 480, 488), and North (1976, pp. 256-257), among others, have commented in a negative fashion on the extent to which the administrative duties of librarians have a deleterious effect on occupational autonomy and authority. Biblartz et al. (1975, p. 127) suggest that the occupation is evolving into a management profession that specializes in libraries. They note that libraries are expanding most at the managerial level of operations (that is, libraries are becoming more bureaucratized). They express the concern that librarians may fail to occupy these positions of authority, allowing them to be filled by nonlibrarians.

These writers either ignore or fail to notice that it is the occupation and not necessarily the organization that is fostering bureaucratic control over library work. Library associations clearly advocate a system of organizational administration as an essential component of occupational authority and control. Adherence to standards of librarianship is conceived to be contingent on librar-ians establishing the appropriate system of formal administration. Bureaucratic mechanisms of control have not been foisted on librarians in every library. In many organizational settings librarians are actively involved in designing the formal system of operations and instituting a regular system of hierarchical supervision and do so under the aegis of occupational standards. Rather than being tarnished by the organizational context of the work setting, the role of librarian as administrator is but one facet in the image of the librarian promoted by the occupation itself.[1]

Organizational Factors

Job descriptions, written records, and the pattern of communication are functions of organizational characteristics as well as occupational orientations. In particular, we found that the size of the circulation, the size of the acquisitions budget, and the type of library were related to these measures of bureaucratic control. The greater the circulation, the more the staff interacted with library users who were unfamiliar with the formal procedures governing library operations. As a consequence, in libraries with larger circulations the staff is likely to accommodate the interests of the users by ignoring their formally prescribed job descriptions (library operations would be debureaucratized). In contrast, libraries with larger acquisitions budgets would be more likely to have written records for reference work. Records documenting the demand for reference service may be used to justify continued financial support. In addition, the general aura of legitimacy associated with a larger budget favors bureaucratization. Public libraries as opposed to business or government libraries are more likely to have supervisory or information-gathering patterns of communication. Librarians have greater autonomy to personally organize and keep track of the work done by their staff in public libraries. In business or government libraries (and to a lesser extent university and college libraries) the superior authority and expertise of many library users limits the librarian's antonomy to organize reference work. Furthermore, the interests of the library itself are often subordinated to the policies, interests, and budgetary practices of the larger organization. Each of these three organizational factors—the size of circulation, the size of the acquisitions budget, and the type of library has a bearing on the existence of bureaucratic control procedures in the library setting.

There are reasons for arguing that these organizational properties alone would not produce the coherent bureaucratic structure favored by the occupation. First, unlike collective orientations toward library associations no single organizational property was correlated with all three indicators of bureaucratic control procedures. Indeed, each indicator of bureaucratic procedures was related to a different organizational factor. Because job descriptions, written records, and communication are functions of different organizational characteristics, they would be unlikely to coexist in any one library unless these different organizational characteristics were positively correlated. This suggests the second reason for arguing that organizational factors would not engender a coherent system of formal control. The relevant organizational characteristics

are not intercorrelated in a way that integrates each distinct bureaucratic procedure into a unified system of control. For example, the size of the acquisitions budget is unrelated either to the size of the circulation or to the type of library. Therefore the use of written records is unlikely to be associated with the existence of
job descriptions or authoritative patterns of communication. The size of the circulation and library type are correlated but in a way that ensures that job descriptions and the pattern of communication are not integrated. Public libraries have the
requisite pattern of communication but experience debureaucratization of job
descriptions because of their larger circulations. In comparison, job descriptions
in business or government libraries are not eroded because their circulations are
small, but they do not possess the appropriate pattern of communication. The
effects of their smaller circulations would be countered by the effects of their
subordinate position in a larger, nonlibrary organization. The negative correlation between the type of library and the size of the circulation reduces the likelihood that job descriptions, written records, and an authoritative pattern of
communication would coexist by chance in any library.

Combined Effects of Occupational and
Organizational Factors

In reality, both occupational and organizational factors operate simultaneously,
with the structure of library work arrangements reflecting the influence of a
composite pattern of factors. Occupational factors are the only ones that have a
coherent effect on library structures. Organizational factors are, at best, unlikely
to produce consistencies and, on occasion, are likely to have inconsistent effects.
A striking demonstration of the inconsistent impact of organizational properties
is revealed when we review the tables and figures that outline the results in
chapters 5 and 6. (See table 8-1 for a summary.) Each indicator of library work
arrangements (not just those representing bureaucratic elements) was a function
of a different set of organizational factors. As a result, it is not surprising that
the system of administration as articulated in library association policies fails
to emerge in any coherent form in any of the libraries surveyed. The piecemeal
effects of organizational factors tended to produce a variety of mutations.
In occupationally oriented library settings these mutations approximate in
different ways and degrees the underlying occupational model of authority and
control over work.

Classical Organizational Theory

In the light of these findings we should be wondering about the extent to which
management plays an active role in the internal administration of organizational
activities. In the classical or rational approach to the study of organizations
internal structure is considered to be solely the product of management planning
and decision making. According to this approach, structures are designed and
controlled by managers to ensure that organizational performance corresponds

with organizational goals. Work settings are organized by supervisors, administrators, and other officials at the managerial level. Managers define the tasks that make up each job or position in the work setting. Job descriptions and directives stipulate how the work is to be done. Management regulates entry into these positions. In order to ascertain an individual's qualifications, management administers tests to determine his or her potential capacity to carry out the assigned work. Task-specific skills are typically learned on the job under the tutelage of a supervisor. Work records maintained by management indicate the performance of each worker. Standards for judging performance are incorporated into the formal job descriptions and directives which, in turn, are ultimately legitimized in terms of the organization's goals.[2]

Job descriptions and written records are regarded as one aspect of a bureaucratic structure of control. Formalization constitutes one possible response by management to problems of integration posed by the size and complexity of operations (the number and diversity of interrelationships to be managed). Administrators rather than workers perform the knowledge-based task of programming solutions to these problems. Coordination of the overall flow of work between formally defined positions and departments takes precedence over discretion exercised by individual workers. Rationality is considered to reside in the organizational structure as designed by management (Mannheim, 1960).

This perspective assumes that "jobs are created, dissolved and reconstituted by management . . . [having] no social or economic foundation for their persistence beyond the plants, agencies or firms in which they exist" (Friedson, 1973, p. 54). Of course, a large number of jobs are part of the task domains claimed by the occupations and professions. Standards and principles articulated by representative associations and schools establish an occupational technology. An occupation's market status is embedded in the educational system of the larger society. To a varying extent occupations and professions have achieved a legal status that enables them to regulate entry as well as to legislate and enforce standards of training and practice. Vested rights may be used by the representative agencies to control the creation and dissemination of knowledge and to create virtual market monopolies. Occupations and professions stand as alternative goal-setting bodies to management vis-à-vis the structuring of work in the organizational setting.[3] Both management and occupational associations may prescribe standards and procedures to be followed in occupational work settings, articulate requisite divisions of labor, specify appropriate flows of communication and information, and designate the legitimate hierarchy of responsibility for particular tasks and work arrangements.

I would like to speculate on the possible parallels that might exist between managerial and occupational authority and control over work. A collective orientation toward either one of these goal-setting bodies would be expected to contribute to the standardization of work arrangements in the setting. Established professions may rely on their market monopoly or their vested rights to regulate and enforce standards of work to produce high levels of occupational orientations; in like fashion, management may manipulate budget allocations or exercise its legal rights to regulate and enforce standards of work to create high levels of collective managerial orientations. However, I suspect that structural power may not be an essential ingredient in managerial authority and control. As in the librarian, management may not be able to wield structural power. Nevertheless, managerial authority and control over work may still manifest itself in managerially oriented settings. Like the literature on the professions, the literature on organizational administration may overemphasize the importance of structural power and influence, giving short shrift to normative, institutional foundations of authority.

Open-System Theory

The focus on management as the prime goal setting body prevails in the open-system approach as well. James Thompson, for example, essentially revamps classical organizational theory to accommodate the open-system approach by expanding the role of management. A rational internal administration is contingent on the management of the flows of inputs and outputs. Formal, bureaucratically controlled operations occur only when management has "control over all the relevant variables or closure" (Thompson, 1967, p. 24). By establishing institutional level agreement on organizational practices (domain consensus) and by mediating the effects of fluctuating inputs and outputs, management determines the extent to which internal administration may be formalized.

To the extent that open-system theorists emphasize the importance of agreement at the institutional level on organizational objectives and technology, this approach may be compatible with the findings of this study. Agreement between senior management and relevant occupational associations on appropriate operating procedures would tend to increase organizational formalization by increasing the level of collective occupational orientations in work settings. Thus chief librarians in public libraries (senior management in public libraries) indirectly influence the structure of authority and control over the flow of work in library settings by endorsing occupational standards of librarianship. The controlling character of these institutions exists over and above any mechanism of sanctions management may employ to sanction compliance (Berger and Luckman, 1966, p. 55).

However, it is not at all obvious that standardization derived from occupational institutions requires that management achieve "control over all relevant variables or closure." I did find evidence that increased contact with library users in the organizational environment tended to debureaucratize internal library operations (that is, libraries with larger circulations were less likely to have job descriptions). But the effects of collective occupational orientations were independent of this process of environmental debureaucratization. In addition, we found that formalization in library settings rarely took the form of a coherent system of bureaucratic control. The existence of job descriptions was unrelated to the existence of written records. If closure is critical and has been achieved, one would expect the resultant capacity of management to plan internal operations on a rational basis would facilitate the development of a coherent system of bureaucratic control. That is, if formalization were contingent on management mediation of the environment, one would expect job descriptions and written records to coexist in library settings. There is no organizational factor that fosters this classical image of management control. Indeed, any coherence between the use of job descriptions and written records could be attributed only to occupational authority and control.

We should revise our image of the role of management in organizations that employ members of an occupation or profession in organizational work settings. In these organizations the management may choose to harness external sources of institutional control by endorsing occupational standards of work. Compliance with occupational norms is contingent on collective orientations in each work setting, not necessarily on the active intervention of management to enforce those standards or to mediate environmental fluctuations. Work in occupationally oriented settings may be quite structured and standardized in organizations whose administrations are relatively small and engage in few of the management strategies deemed necessary to run a tight operation.

Notes

1. Studies of scientists, engineers, and other technical experts who work in organizational settings have revealed that promotion into management positions is often regarded as a mark of professional success (Goldner and Ritti, 1967; Goldberg, 1976, pp. 337-338; Perrow, 1979, pp. 50-55). However, these studies have gathered data on the personal orientations of practitioners rather than on the policies and standards articulated by the associations and schools that define the occupation's task domain. We do not know whether these personal orientations are reflections of occupational institutions or whether they are merely personal adaptations to working in an organizational setting. Perrow does speculate that the university training received by members of these occupations is vocationally oriented. The implication is that once on the job, graduates of these programs would see no inherent conflict between advancement into the managerial hierarchy and occupational norms and may even be encouraged by their training to regard such advancement as consistent with professional success.

2. See, for example, Simon (1957).

3. In addition to senior management and occupational or profressional associations, a list of potential goal-setting bodies for an organization might include a board of directors, staff planners, unions, certain government agencies, and even companies that design elaborate machinery for organizational use.

10 Occupational Orientations Shape Organizational Structure, Not Vice Versa

The central argument has been that occupational standards mold library work arrangements in occupationally oriented settings. Collective occupational orientations shape organizational structure by providing a climate favorable to the exercise of occupational authority. This argument runs counter to the general proposition that the structure of a person's immediate context determines his or her values and beliefs. Most variants of this general proposition cannot account for the findings of this study.

Instead of attempting to explain the structure of work arrangements, this chapter turns the tables and investigates possible explanations for occupational orientations and occupational standards. Certain contextual properties of libraries may have a bearing on orientations. However, both the structural power of the occupation and the standardization of library operations are rejected as determinants of occupational orientations. The second and last part of this chapter is devoted to a consideration of the relationship between work carried out in libraries and the policies adopted by library associations. The conclusion reached is that association policies are a synthesis of occupational standards and principles, a synthesis that is achieved outside libraries in response to political processes. As such, these policies are independent creations that may or may not reflect actual work practices in typical libraries.

Collective Occupational Orientation

Structural Foundations of the Occupation

While the structural powers of the established professions may virtually guarantee that their members work in occupationally oriented settings, such is not the case for librarians. The librarian occupation was chosen for study in large part because it lacked the structural power associated with legally vested rights or with a market monopoly and yet had representative associations and schools that enunciated occupational standards and principles. Were library associations to have the right to certify librarians, to enforce a code of ethics, or to enter into contractual negotiations on their behalf, these associations might be able to enforce compliance with occupational standards and procedures. However, as of 1974, the date of the survey, library associations did not possess any of these powers commonly associated with a profession. Neither the library associations nor the library schools could demand the adoption of a particular style of work; they could not pressure libraries to copy the standardized arrangements that they advocated in their policies. As library associations do not possess the power to bolster the authority of individual librarians, interaction between the authority of librarians and the power of library associations would be nonexistent. By choosing to study only one occupation, the main effects of structural power from one work setting to another are held constant (structural power would vary from one occupation to another, not from one work setting to another in the same legal jurisdictions). Should collective orientation toward the librarian occupation be found to be correlated with standardized work arrangements in library settings, this result could not be attributed to the structural power of the occupation.

In full-fledged professions or in craft unions for that matter, the institutional expertise exercised by practitioners is backed by the structural power of such occupations. Collective orientation in work settings toward the occupation would virtually assure that collective orientation would be relatively high in all organizational settings employing its members. (See figure 2-1.) The degree of collective orientation toward the occupation would not vary appreciably from one work setting to another. The lack of variance in the independent variable would frustrate any statistical analysis of the effects of institutional occupational control.

Contextual Properties of Libraries as Organizations

Library staff in some settings, but not others, may be encouraged to regard the librarian occupation as the reference group most relevant to their work. For example, collective occupational orientations are higher in libraries with greater numbers of librarians and larger acquisitions budgets. These organizational characteristics may have an indirect effect on the standardization of library operations by fostering occupational orientations which, in turn, establish an occupational structure of authority and control in the setting. (See figure 8-1.) However, this argument accounts for only some of the results, those vis-à-vis written records, consensus on role expectations for library assistants, and the pattern of communication. There is no evidence that the organizational context molds work orientations or indirectly affects the use of job descriptions, consensus on role expectations for library clerks, or specialist role expectations.

Indeed, there is evidence that the size of the circulation, the number of full-time positions, and the presence of library assistants (nonspecialized staff) actually suppresses the relationship between occupational orientations and library work arrangements. Job descriptions, consensus on role expectations, and specialist role expectations for librarians and library assistants tend to exist in libraries with smaller circulations, fewer full-time staff, and no library assistants, respectively. Yet libraries with smaller circulations, fewer staff, and no library assistants tend not to be oriented toward library associations and the librarian occupation. The effects of these contextual properties of the organization on the structure of library work arrangements is not mediated by the occupational orientations of the staff.

There is no support for the hypothesis that threats to occupational autonomy or the occupational composition of senior management accounts for the correlation between orientation and the structure of work arrangements. A number of writers on professionalism have argued that the degree of bureaucratization in the larger organizational context influences occupational orientations by threatening professional autonomy (Hall, 1968; Scott, 1965) or the professional ideal of service (Wilensky, 1964). From another perspective, the occupational composition of the dominant coalition in control of the larger organization may be expected to provide a reference group that would influence occupational orientations. In her study of identity among pharmacists Kronus concluded that "occupational identification appears to flourish (or survive) only in the *absence* of a powerful organizational framework that presents alternative [i.e., nonoccupational] rewards or pressures" (1976b, p. 325).

The type of library seems to represent both the existence of a threat to occupational autonomy and the existence of a reference group in senior management. In public libraries the threat of outside intervention in library operations was low, and senior management was almost invariably drawn from the ranks of librarians. In business and government libraries the threat was higher, and librarians were relegated to a staff position and denied opportunities for advancement into the line of command. University and college libraries would be ranked between public libraries, on the one hand, and business and government libraries, on the other. While librarians did not advance into the positions of dean, vice-president, or president, they did manage the administration that controlled the day-to-day operation of the library. The threat of outside intervention existed but was generally lower than in libraries attached to businesses or government departments. The existence of two distinct reference groups—librarians in middle management and the academic staff—introduced a note of ambiguity in the orientations of library staff (Schroeder, 1975) that would not be present in public libraries.

Occupational orientations were correlated with the type of library but not in a way that would account for the correlation between occupational orientations and the structure of work arrangements. The pattern of communication and the use of job descriptions depended on the type of library. However, collective occupational orientations and the type of library had statistically independent effects on the pattern of communication (figure 7-1). With regard to the use of job descriptions, the larger circulations of public libraries accounted for the relative absence of job descriptions in their work settings. If the type of library had any effect, it was to suppress the relationship between occupational orientations and the use of job descriptions (figure 6-3). Although the type of library did affect occupational orientations in the predicted direction, this factor cannot account for the effect that occupational orientations appeared to have on library work arrangements.

Thus the results are somewhat inconclusive. Some but not all organizational properties may influence orientations in ways that account for some of the results. Furthermore, even where it can be shown that the organizational context encourages occupational orientations, the results suggest that authority and control over work in the organization are modeled on occupational standards of librarianship.

Standardized Work Arrangements

The most consistent pattern in the survey results was the positive correlation between occupational orientations and standardization of work arrangements. Occupational orientations have been regarded as the factor that contributes to standardization. Could it be that the causal ordering is actually reversed, that standardization shapes orientations of the library staff rather than vice versa?

The Temporal Sequence of Events. In its simplest form this proposition may merely be claiming that most job descriptions, systems of written records, role expectations, and patterns of communications that existed in the library settings in 1974 probably predated the employment of most of the library staff. The occupational orientations of the library staff in 1974 could not possibly account for the structure of library practices instituted at a much earlier time. On the other hand, work arrangements created in the past could influence the orientations of the current staff. For the moment let us consider only the temporal order of the variables and not the more basic question how work arrangements per se might produce occupational orientations. The level of collective occupational orientations and the structure of library operations are probably constant over time. For example, the level of collective occupational orientations tends to remain stable so long as there are no major shifts in the number or proportion of librarians on the staff or the level of financial support received by the library. Changes induced by occupational orientations probably occur on an incremental basis throughout the history of the organization as well as during periods of initial organization or reorganization. There would be a steady pressure to increase the alignment between library procedures and occupational institutions. Similarly, the structure of library work arrangements would remain constant so long as there were no significant changes in the occupational composition of the setting or in the size of library operations. The current correlation between occupational orientations and the structure of library work arrangements probably reflects the correlation that emerged during the initial organization of the library or during the last period of major reorganization or rapid growth. It is the temporal sequence of events during those periods of change that is of greatest importance. Only a historical analysis of events during periods of change would let us know whether changes in the level of occupational orientations were followed by changes in the work arrangements or vice versa.

The Invisible Correlation. Although we do not have historical data, we may reevaluate the data yielded by the survey to assess whether it is plausible to presume that work arrangements shape occupational orientations. If work arrangements per se suggest the "correct" orientations (the orientations to which new members of staff would be expected to conform), one would expect the correlation between those work arrangements and occupational orientations to be obvious and well known to informed participants. In fact, the findings of this study were not common knowledge among those who worked in the library settings surveyed. On being told about the strong and consistent correlation between standardization and occupational orientations, librarians invariably expressed surprise. This correlation was not at all obvious to them.

The surprised reaction of librarians to the results may be traced, in part, to the fact that these variables were in fact constants within the vast majority of the settings. (Only one library was in the process of a major reorganization.) The level of collective awareness of library associations varied from being almost totally absent in some settings to being omnipresent in others. However, within any one setting the level of collective awareness would not vary appreciably over time. For all intents and purposes this factor would be regarded by most as a constant rather than as a variable. For similar reasons, conditions of work in the experience of most would also be constant rather than variable. The experience of those working in these libraries tended to be limited to one library (or one type and size of library). Library staff were simply not familiar with the contrasts that existed between one library and another. As a consequence, most seemed to presume that other libraries were essentially similar to their own, that certain basic understandings and formats regarding library work were universally present in all library settings. Because most personnel would not have witnessed any change in collective awareness or in the standardization of norms and role expectations, let alone the covariation of these two variables, the connection between collective awareness and standardization would not be apparent.

In participant observation studies a common test of the validity of the researcher's interpretation of the results is to determine whether the analysis is meaningful for respondents in the setting. However, seeking the reactions of respondents to the results of this study may not be a fair test of their validity. Perhaps all that should be expected is that the measures entered into a multivariate analysis should be meaningful to the respondents. In this regard the results of this study have validity. Care was taken to ensure that the unit of analysis was a recognizable, concrete entity for respondents. (See appendix A.) Because most questions were made specific to the task and the situation the information being sought was not hypothetical. For many questions two respondents were able to pool their impressions of a correct answer; their discussions revealed that the questions were meaningful to them. The high rate of cooperation, setting by setting and item by item, demonstrates that the questions were meaningful to them. The validity of the results of a multivariate analysis may be better assessed at a theoretical level.

Even if most library personnel had witnessed changes in the levels of occupational orientations or standardization, it is still unlikely that they would see the correlation between these two variables. Library work arrangements do not possess the logical integrity and coherence to mold orientations. There is no single philosophy of work or source of inspiration imbedded in the structure of operations in any one of the libraries surveyed. Each of the indicators of standardization was a function of a number of different organizational characteristics, not just occupational orientations. Work arrangement constitutes an amalgamation of a number of different forces.

If most phenomena are caused by several factors, it may be unwarranted to expect library staff to be able to recognize the independent effects of any single factor in their setting. First, some variables such as the number or proportion of librarians on the staff and the dollar value of the acquisitions budget represented active factors in the setting. While the level of collective occupational orientations is taken for granted as a constant, the staff paid attention to important reference groups and to their budgets as important causal agents that determined their fate in the organization. If the staff was able to see any correlation between the structure of their work arrangements and other factors, they would be much more likely to attribute variations in their conditions of work to changes in the occupational composition of the setting or to changes in their budget. Of course, this interpretation would be spurious to the extent that it failed to recognize the independent effect of occupational orientations. However, that is just the point. It is easy for the participant observer to have spurious interpretations of correlations.

Second, other factors such as the number of materials circulated, the number of full-time staff, and the presence of library assistants had the effect of suppressing the correlation between standardization and occupational orientation. The effects of occupational orientations on job descriptions and occupational role expectations were "washed out" by the contrary effects of these organizational properties. Given the mixture of these opposing processes, even a trained observer who was aware of the results of the regression analyses would be unable to see any correlation between the work arrangements and any of these suppressed factors.

Third, each indicator of occupational work arrangements was a function of different sets of factors. While occupational orientations were consistently correlated with each measure of work arrangements, the relevant organizational characteristics were not. Job descriptions, written records, consensus on role expectations, specialist role expectations, and supervisory patterns of communication did not coexist as a coherent package of occupational practices in any one of the libraries surveyed. The contextual properties of libraries as organizations served to fragment occupational work arrangements, producing varying combinations of these structures in each setting. In practice, library work arrangements were organized on a piecemeal basis and did not reflect a single, coherent philosophy or set of standards. Both the quantitative results and the qualitative impressions provided by the survey indicate that rationality behind library operative procedures was not so obvious that it could be inductively grasped by a library's staff and influence their orientations in a consistent or coherent fashion. It is one thing to suggest that the staff conforms to the orientations of an important reference group actually present in the work setting. It is quite another to argue that the staff can divine the institutional orientations of their setting on their own, without guidance from others.

Occupational Standards and Library
Work Arrangements

If it is unlikely that work arrangements per se shape occupational orientations within library settings, is it possible that these organizational structures influence the policies of library associations? Could the connection between occupational standards and organizational structures originate in the organizations rather than in the associations, given the participation of practicing librarians in the formulation of library association policies? This is not to suggest that the forty-six librarians interviewed in Alberta participated in the formulation of the relevant ALA and CLA policies; most of these policies antedate the careers of these librarians. The question is whether practicing librarians en masse determine the problem addressed and solutions proposed by library associations, thereby keeping standards of librarianship in line with current library practices.

Do library associations merely highlight existing practices within organizations? This is an interesting question, one that touches on the discussion of innovative libraries. The four innovative libraries identified in chapter 6 were collectively oriented toward the occupation to an extraordinary degree. Practicing librarians did participate in library association; the chief librarians in two of the four had recently been top executives in a central library association. The interesting point is that the work arrangements in these four innovative libraries did not conform to occupational standards and they eschewed all forms of formal regulation. The rationale for this discrepancy given by those in charge was that their libraries were unique and that the standard occupational prescriptions were not appropriate guides for their library's operations. Thus these practicing librarians who participated in the inner councils of library associations clearly differentiated between the organizational structures in their libraries and the occupational standards articulated by the library associations and they indicated no desire to modify the latter to conform to the former.

The survey of the professional literature of the librarian occupation suggests that the process of setting occupational standards is not simply one of aggregating existing organizational practices or providing a showcase for existing model libraries. Occupational standards represent a social construction of reality. Berger and Luckman would refer to them as first- and second-order objectifications of reality (1966, pp. 92-104). Three conditions tended to favor this interpretation and this allusion to Berger and Luckman. (1) Only a small minority of the interviewed librarians regularly attended professional meetings or possessed a detailed knowledge of policy considerations of library associations. (2) A great deal of concern in the professional literature was directed toward integrating new proposals into the existing body of knowledge, principles, and policies of library associations and schools of library science. In particular, ALA and CLA policy statements on reference service and the acquisition of new materials, the two tasks analyzed in detail, were devoid of any reference to existing organizational practices. (3) In addition, a comparison of 1948 ALA policy on reference service and the acquisition of new materials with statements in the early 1970s revealed that change has been minimal. This is so despite the fact that the expansion of media services and the rise of library technicians has threatened the hegemony enjoyed by librarians. Policy seems to lag behind practice. Even if those associations or schools should respond to issues raised by practicing librarians, that input would be transformed by the staff within those associations and schools before reemerging as policy output. These policies represent a synthesis with existing doctrine and, in some instances, politically motivated compromise. As I envisage this process, input from practicing librarians might initiate a review of occupational standards. In turn, new standards would tend to be incorporated at some subsequent date in occupationally oriented libraries. This would most likely occur in new libraries or in existing libraries during periods of substantial growth and reorganization. It is not at all obvious that newly promulgated occupational standards would closely resemble current work arrangements of practicing librarians. Thus it is unlikely that the results are the product of practicing librarians' setting both occupational policies and organizational structures.

Conclusions

Collective occupational orientations are positively correlated with the presence of librarians in the work setting and the level of financial support received by the library. Each of these contextual properties appears to have an indirect effect on standardization of library operations by affecting collective occupational orientations. Other factors such as the structural power of the occupation or standardized conditions of work do not provide plausible explanations for variations in the level of collective occupational orientations. In addition, it seems more likely that occupational standards inspired standardization in library work settings than vice versa. The basic proposition that occupational standards affect library work arrangements in occupationally oriented settings remains the most plausible explanation for the results of the survey.

**Part IV
A Theory of
Occupational Authority**

11 Occupational Authority

Collective Occupational Orientation

By articulating a knowledge base that details how work is to be done, library associations create the institutional foundations necessary for occupational authority. These institutions are accepted as defining work arrangements in settings collectively oriented toward the occupation as represented by these associations. An orientation toward the occupation seems to denote a predisposition to rely on other librarians and the professional literature for guidance when dealing with a problem. Most librarians did not possess a detailed knowledge of current standards published by library associations. Although collective occupational orientations do not denote widespread technical expertise or knowledge of occupational standards, they are indicative of a readiness to accept work arrangements explicitly justified in terms of occupational institutions as social norms. In these circumstances social norms would encourage librarians to organize work of others as well as themselves in accordance with their understanding of their occupation's standards.

Occupational standards tend to have the status of social norms in occupationally oriented settings. As social norms, these standards derive their controlling character from two sources: the appearance of unanimous acceptance by those in the work setting (Asch, 1958) and the tendency of individuals in the setting to punish behavior that departs from the ideal (Homans, 1950, pp. 121-128). The willingness of individuals to act on personal conviction in their dealings with others, including their willingness to sanction the behavior of others, is tempered by their perception of social support in the setting (Asch, 1958). Collective occupational orientations reflect the extent to which there will be an appearance of unanimous acceptance of occupational standards and a perception that social support exists within the setting for their enforcement.

Normatively oriented behavior is not necessarily inner-directed behavior.[1] Librarians may possess a high level of training and may have internalized occupational rules of conduct and yet be unwilling to act on those personal beliefs in settings that are not collectively oriented toward the occupation. If occupational standards do not have the status of social norms, proceeding to organize work in accordance with those standards would not only meet with little cooperation but would also run the risk of violating existing social norms, provoking collective resistance from others. Becker and Geer (1958), in their article entitled "The Fate of Idealism in Medical School," observed that senior medical students suppressed any expression or even thoughts of idealism regarding professional service when in the presence of their colleagues. Not only was idealism regarded as deviant in this social setting, but it was irrelevant to group activities in their medical program. Becker and Geer's example demonstrates that occupational groups can influence individuals to keep deviant thoughts to themselves. Librarians in libraries not oriented toward their occupation would tend to avoid any expression or thought of occupational standards if these were regarded as deviant or irrelevant to group activities. In accommodating themselves to existing social norms, librarians would be more likely to hold their internalized standards of conduct in abeyance or even to discard them as irrelevant while in inhospitable circumstances.

In their dealings with members of the support staff, clients, or employers, librarians define work situations in terms of occupational status expectations only if the others are collectively oriented toward their occupation. All those who actively participate in the work setting must be aware of and share in the collective orientation toward the occupation. Each participant accepts the occupational orientation in the belief that everyone else in the situation does so as well. Under these conditions one can continue to participate only if one does so in accordance with the institutions of the relevant occupation. The complex of occupational values and beliefs is fused with local norms and role expectations, becoming social imperatives in the work setting (Williams, 1960). It is the conjunction of well-defined institutional foundations outside the setting and the collective orientation toward those foundations inside the setting that establishes the authority of individual librarians.

The Enforcement of Occupational Authority in the Work Setting

The institutions ascribe various qualities to members of the dominant occupation, to those in ancillary positions, and to clients and employers insofar as they are involved in the task domain. The status distinctions are drawn most sharply between members of the dominant occupation and the others. Where lines of jurisdiction prescribe a clear division of labor, the skills and knowledge ascribed to librarians are considered to be more essential to the success of joint endeavors. Where those in ancillary positions perform duties delegated to them by librarians, status distinctions emphasize the librarian's greater breadth of competence. Their repertoire of skills would be judged to be more extensive, their knowledge and sense of purpose, more comprehensive.

Collective occupational orientations are relevant to the authority of the librarian because these orientations indicate that relationships of superiority and inferiority in the setting are modeled on occupational institutions and that nonlibrarians as well as librarians subscribe to that model of authority.

The status situation within the setting tends to correspond to the occupational status order as represented by library associations. Weber (1946, pp. 186-187) designates as a " 'status situation' every typical component of the life fate of men that is determined by a specific, positive or negative, social estimation of *honor.*" Where collective occupational orientations create agreement on social ranks in the work setting, behavioral reactions to their common status expectations create a power differential favoring the person accorded the greater status. Individuals with subordinate status tend to defer to members of the dominant occupation. Members of the dominant status are given more opportunities to initiate interaction in the setting. In turn, members of the dominant status are likely to take the initiative because, within the occupation's task domain, they tend to regard the others as inferior to themselves. In the event of a disagreement between statuses, those in the dominant occupation are unlikely to alter their stance on an issue, while those in a subordinate status would be more likely to change (Torrance, 1954). Status expectations create a power differential in accordance with the hierarchy of dominance as envisaged in occupational institutions.

If authority is taken to mean the legitimate exercise of power, it is argued that both power and legitimacy—authority—can be derived from the normative foundations of an occupation. By affecting status expectations, occupational institutions provide an interpersonal source of power on the job for members of the dominant occupation. In comparison with power derived from the structural foundations outside the work setting, the source of normatively based power is engendered within the work setting. Power is a product of status expectations held within the setting; the legitimacy of this power is a product of the consonance between those status expectations and occupational institutions. It is apparent that the librarian must conform to the standards of his or her occupation in order to maintain both power and legitimacy on the job. Occupational institutions channel and constrain as well as motivate those with authority (Lehman, 1969). Exercising status-based power in accordance with occupational standards and principles is the essence of occupational authority.

This image of occupational authority stresses the importance of normative foundations—occupational institutions—as a basis for status expectations within work settings. In contrast, the existence of structural foundations—the capacity of the occupation to enforce its standards—is not an essential ingredient of occupational authority. It is at this point that our argument diverges from Friedson's perspective on the nature of professional authority. He states, that "on a broad, societal level, . . . a profession must persuade the sovereign of its competence" (Friedson, 1970, pp. 122-123). The support of the state enables the occupation to enforce its standards through any one of a number of legal, educational and economic processes. It is likely that occupations with the power to enforce standards would engender a pervasive and omnipresent orientation toward the occupation in most if not all work settings. By reinforcing status expectations that correspond to occupational institutions, powerful structural foundations would buttress the normative processes on which occupational authority rests. However, rather than being regarded as a necessary condition for occupational authority, powerful structural foundations are considered to be only a sufficient condition for high levels of collective occupational orientation. In the case of the librarian occupation, the impact of occupational institutions on library work arrangements could not be attributed to any structurally based power to enforce occupational standards.

The Reinforcement of Occupational Authority

If the behavior of the librarian conforms to occupational standards, it is most unlikely that subsequent interpersonal experience will modify status expectations in the work setting. In the course of acting out their institutionalized roles, librarians would symbolically emphasize the continuing relevance of occupational institutions in the setting. According to the policies of library associations, librarians must establish the detailed policies that shape and guide the type of library service to be provided. They alone should set up the library's table of organization to achieve those policies, assigning tasks to be performed by ancillary occupations and reserving for themselves the central tasks as professional duties. Librarians should create systems of records and statistics and should arrange for close supervision of their staff. The right to interpret and evaluate these data rests with librarians. Any delegation of these responsibilities that would impair the librarian's preeminence within the work setting is deemed to be unprofessional. By following the edicts of their occupation to direct and supervise the actions of others, librarians institute work arrangements that have the effect of consolidating and entrenching their power. Furthermore, they tend to direct the work toward their areas of expertise. As a consequence, the performance of the librarian in the work setting is more often than not demonstrably superior to that of others in the setting. By behaving consistently within the bounds prescribed by the occupational institutions and by acting from a sense of conviction based on those institutions, the librarian makes the status expectations in the setting self-fulfilling prophecies. The actual pattern of behavior confirms the reality and hence validates the institutional status order.

The correct performance of their prescribed roles by those in authority creates "demand effects" in the work setting (Orne and Evans, 1965; Milgram, 1965). To the extent that those in subordinate statuses have some appreciation of specific principles or rules of conduct, the compliance of subordinate statuses may be active as well as passive. In his study of work settings within a psychiatric hospital Rushing (1964) found that members of subordinate occupations often had difficulty in managing role conflicts created by ambiguously defined duties. He cited an example involving social workers who reduced such role conflict by taking the initiative in proposing standardized procedures that routinized demands for their services. They obtained agreement on role expectations by using the ideas of their supervisors, resident medical doctors, to legitimize their proposals (they defined their roles in terms of the other's self-interests). The residents tended to acquiesce to job descriptions, written records, or other forms of standardized role expectations if they corresponded to the standards and principles of their occupation. Demand effects reinforced the formal system of authority in the organization.

While librarians are presumed to be knowledgeable about most occupational practices and principles, the others in the setting need not be. In fact, their very ignorance tends to reinforce the occupational structure of authority in the setting. Members of the dominant occupation know what they are doing and what they are talking about, and others in the work setting do not. The standard expectancies of subordinates are based on second-hand learning from their superiors rather than on their own trials and errors. Garfinkel (1964, p. 245) noted that

> ... *attributed* standardization ... is supported by the fact that persons avoid the very situations in which they might learn about them. Lay as well as professional knowledge ... is prominently based on ... such procedure. Indeed, the more important the rule, the greater ... the likelihood that knowledge is based on avoided tests.

Subordinates go out of their way to avoid challenging the authority of members of the dominant occupation. Faced with the relatively blind obedience of clients and of workers in ancillary positions, librarians are obliged by the ethics of their occupation to take responsibility for their actions. In carrying out this duty they provide detailed directives, instructions, and job descriptions to ensure that those under them knew what to do, when to do it, and how to do it. Close supervision and written records may also be used to determine whether such task prescriptions were effective. As well as consolidating and entrenching occupationally based power, these actions would formalize work arrangements in the setting.

During the survey librarians often intimated that library clerks were ignorant. They suggested that the clerks did not understand the larger system of library operations within which they worked. Clerks themselves confessed that they might not be knowledgeable or competent enough to answer the questionnaire. They often attributed their uneasiness to their lack of familiarity with the principles of librarianship and library science. It became apparent that these clerks presumed that the object of the survey was to study the application of those principles. Nonlibrarians frequently confused this survey with student questionnaires they had received in the past. The School of Library Science at the University of Alberta required that their students complete data-based projects. The purpose of student surveys was usually to study the application of principles of library science. In conversations with librarians it was mentioned that many of these questionnaires could be understood only by librarians and then only because they had been in library school themselves. Occupationally oriented libraries received more than their fair share of these student questionnaires. The receipt of student questionnaires had the effect of reaffirming the occupational status superiority of the librarian within the setting. Perhaps in the light of their experiences with student questionnaires, nonlibrarians, especially clerks, expected that the librarian would be the only one able to provide adequate answers on any library survey, including this one. In the absence of any experience or information to the contrary the clerks seemed to presume that librarians as an occupational group possessed a societal monopoly on wisdom with respect to library service. (Other nonprofessionals may have voiced such reservations as well. However, in retrospect, the stance of clerks was most vivid.)

The position of the librarian vis-à-vis the library clerk was quite different in settings that were not collectively oriented toward the occupation. Individual clerks were often identified by the librarian in charge as being particularly well informed about various aspects of the library's operations, past and present. In some cases these clerks were explicitly acknowledged to be as knowledgeable as the librarian about the interests of library users and about the purposes behind library procedures. These clerks were personally familiar with most of the people who used the library, knew the types of books and magazines they wanted, and could advise them on where such materials might be located in the library. Expertise in these settings seemed to be based on past experience and seniority within the work setting. To the extent that library clerks had greater experience or seniority than the librarian, authority was divorced from official rank and position.

In occupationally oriented setting librarians never deferred to the seniority or experience of their clerks. Doubts about the ability of clerks to properly carry out their duties without guidance and supervision were explicitly expressed by some librarians. (No recollection exists of any sub-rosa comments of this nature in settings not oriented toward the librarian occupation.) Consideration of local experience and seniority receded and was replaced by a sense of expertise based on the knowledge of the principles of librarianship. The authority of librarians was legitimized in terms of the institutions of librarianship. Ignorance was interpreted not as a lack of access to sources of local information, but rather as symptomatic of the lack of professional training. According to the local wisdom accepted by both librarians and nonlibrarians, it was due to their lack of professional training that nonlibrarians passed on nonroutine tasks to librarians or sought the approval of librarians before doing such tasks themselves, deferring to judgments expressed by librarians. Similarly, librarians took responsibility for supervising and regulating the work of nonlibrarians because their subordinates lacked professional training. Such librarians suspected that nonlibrarians really did not know what they were doing, librarians were motivated to maintain some form of supervision, to use written records, and to set up job descriptions. The more the qualifications of subordinates diverged from the professional norm—a general baccalaureate, postgraduate training in library work, on-the-job experience in a good library—the more librarians felt moved to formally organize and supervise their work. Perhaps more important, nonlibrarians themselves were motivated to comply fully with such arrangements because they felt that the librarians were the experts.

While librarians may not possess a societal monopoly over a knowledge base, in occupationally oriented settings they tended to have a monopoly over relevant information within the confines of the library. Objectively, this monopoly seemed to be the product of work arrangements that corresponded with occupational standards and principles. In library settings oriented toward the occupation librarians took the initiative in keeping in touch with others. In the process of consulting and supervising others librarians became aware of most events and developments in their setting. Thus not only were librarians familiar with the formal systems of regulation, they also occupied the central position in the local system of communication. Subjectively, everyone in occupationally oriented settings was aware of the knowledge differential that separated librarians from nonlibrarians. When asked to account for this differential, each seemed to presume that the librarian occupation had a societal monopoly over a specialized body of knowledge. The greater knowledge of librarians was attributed to their professional training, a quality that emphasized the privileged status of the librarian in relation to that specialized body of knowledge. The reality of the knowledge differential was interpreted in terms of universal occupational institutions rather than in terms of the centralized nature of the work arrangements in the particular library. Because librarians in occupationally oriented settings tended to enjoy a monopoly over relevant information within the library, the question of whether or not their occupation also possessed a societal monopoly on knowledge was never raised as an issue. Thus in library settings oriented toward their occupation, the structure of the work arrangements instituted by librarians had the effect of validating the authority imputed to them.

Standardized Work Arrangements

Standardized work arrangements are artifacts of occupational authority and control. Librarians, in particular, are enjoined by library associations to establish formal systems of library administration. However, there are reasons to believe that standardization would emerge in occupationally oriented settings even in the absence of specific prescriptions to formalize library operations.

Occupational institutions provide a definition of the situation that enables role expectations to be understood on a more explicit basis, stabilizing mutual expectations and creating consensus on the competence and responsibilities of incumbents of each occupational status. Institutionalized work arrangements are impersonal in that they exemplify practices that are widely adopted elsewhere. The authority structure, division of labor, job qualifications, and rights and responsibilities conform to standards and principles devised outside the work setting rather than reflect procedures developed in the setting on the basis of personal experience. The institutionalization of expertise and authority is denoted by the standardization of work arrangements. The expert's response to ignorance in subordinates or clients is to formalize his transactions with them and to routinize the system of administration and supervision.

The structure of work arrangements associated with the occupational authority of the librarian has many of the characteristics associated with the bureaucratic authority of an administration. Perrow (1979, pp. 50-55) questions the distinction drawn between authority based on technical competence and authority based on the office held. The arguments and evidence presented in this study substantiate his contention that the two forms of authority are not mutually exclusive bases of organization. Like a bureaucratic hierarchy of authority, the occupational dominance order prescribed by library associations centralizes the authority to plan and regulate library work in the hands of the librarian. Both the members of the dominant occupation and the bureaucrat derive their authority from the competence and responsibility imputed to them by others.[2] That is, the librarian's competence and responsibilities are demarcated by library associations and reaffirmed on the job by the deference of status inferiors. Similarly, the bureaucrats' competence and responsibilities are demarcated by senior management and reaffirmed on the job by the deference of subordinates. Like the official whose rationality is lodged in organizational institutions and structures, the rationality of the librarian is imbedded in occupational institutions and work arrangements. Most librarians interviewed in the survey could not articulate policies of library associations that were relevant to the actual practices of their particular library. Even though an analysis of the survey data revealed that these policies were correlated with work arrangements in occupationally oriented settings, librarians were not cognizant of this fact. Both members of the dominant occupation and bureaucrats rely on their position to monopolize the flow of information in the work setting. By using an esoteric system of categorization to classify individual cases and problems and by insisting on the right to withhold information, both establish a sense of social distance that limits the ability of others to evaluate their expertise. Thus occupational authority and control is associated with formalized and standardized conditions of work; it is also marked by an occupational dominance order in the work setting that resembles a bureaucratic system of authority and control.

Notes

1. By explicitly seeking the personal orientations of a librarian, the interviewer may be implicitly encouraging the librarian to report convictions that are not shared with others on the staff. If those personal orientations are not sanctioned as social norms, there could be an even greater discrepancy between personal beliefs and values reported to an outside interviewer and the convictions expressed and acted on when working with members of the library staff. We cannot assume that the personal occupational orientation of the librarian is indicative of the extent to which nonlibrarians in the work setting endorse the occupational model of authority.

2. Friedson makes much the same argument when discussing the authority of the physician. "On the level of practice, competence is merely an imputation to the status of the individual professional, a status similar to that of the bureaucratic official" (Friedson, 1970, pp. 122-123).

12 Conclusions

The system of library administration prescribed by central library associations tended to exist in library settings collectively oriented toward those associations. Librarians were encouraged to institute bureaucratic mechanisms of control in the work setting: job descriptions, written records, and a centralized system of personal information gathering and supervision. This system of administration ensured that the librarian was the dominant occupation in the library, and it enabled the librarian to organize the reference service provided to the library's clientele. It also furnished the librarian with a virtual monopoly over the flow and interpretation of information about current library operations. This monopoly over information heightened the awareness of occupational status distinctions and reaffirmed the authority of the librarian.

Control over work in settings oriented toward library associations is locally enforced. Library associations and schools of library science do not have the power to control entry into the occupation. Without an effective monopoly over occupational services, without the recognition and support of the state, and without a capacity to take collective action, the occupation is unable to enforce compliance with occupational standards of practice. Nevertheless, both the form and the formality of work practices in library settings were associated with a collective orientation toward library associations. Occupational control over work arrangements in library settings exists even though the librarian occupation lacks the structural powers possessed by established professions and craft unions.

Normative foundations outside the setting and normative orientations within the setting combine to create a locally enforced system of order. In addition to providing an explanation for the librarian's occupational authority and control over library work, this theory should be relevant to other occupations and professions that have a well-defined task domain and technology. For technical occupations and semiprofessions that cannot enforce occupational standards one would expect results similar to those found in this study. The level of occupational orientations would vary from one setting to another; the higher the collective orientations toward the occupation, the more the status of the practitioner would correspond to the ideals of the occupation and the greater the similarity between actual work practices and standards of work. Although the process would be much the same in the established professions, the results would be different. Given the legal or economic power to enforce standards, occupational orientations would tend to be uniformly high in the various settings in which their members work. If occupational orientations did not vary from one setting to another, it would be impossible to demonstrate that standardization of work arrangements covaried with occupational orientation. (It was for this reason that such an occupation was not studied.) However, in terms of the results of this study, it would be predicted that work arrangements would be standardized in accordance with occupational norms in most if not all settings. All practitioners would enjoy a relatively high level of occupational authority. On a day-to-day basis it seems reasonable to presume that the structural power of the professional association would merely reinforce the local enforcement of professional standards.

Speculations

Perhaps this is the point at which to speculate on the possible wider significance of this study. First, it seems that local enforcement of institutional standards would occur in nonorganizational as well as in organizational work settings. Occupational institutions provide both a source of power and a source of legitimacy in occupationally oriented work settings. For example, the authority of the professional in private practice exists without the backing of a managerial bureaucracy. Similarly, craftsmen in the construction industry exercise authority on the work site that is essentially unrelated to the administrative work carried out by the contractor. This study found no evidence that the occupational authority and control over library work depended on factors conventionally associated with the existence of an administrative staff at the managerial level outside the work setting. The endorsement of the occupation's task domain by the management of an organization does not seem to be critical to the process. As envisaged, any authority or discretion delegated by higher level management to members of the dominant occupation in an organizational work setting would only supplement occupationally based authority.

Second, the local enforcement of institutional standards may be associated with all types of corporately organized status groups, not just with corporately organized occupational status groups. "Work" need not refer solely to endeavor in the economic system; work refers to the application of the joint efforts of several individuals to some purpose. The associations that represent the interests of such status groups may define the task domain as well as a distinctive style of work or technology for living to be carried out in that domain. For example, women's groups have succeeded in articulating a technology for living that benefits a "liberated" woman. On the basis of my results, standardized arrangements modeled on those institutions should emerge in families ("work settings") collectively oriented toward that status group as represented by women's associations. The locally enforced system of order is explained by the conjunction of normative foundations outside the setting and normative orientations within the setting.

Summary of the Argument

The occupational institutions articulated by representative associations and training schools are an essential part of occupational authority in work settings. By labeling the participants and typifying the activities carried out in the occupation's task domain, library associations define conventional work situations, providing a source of guidance on correct procedures and practices. Among those familiar with the vernacular of library associations and schools, this definition can be used to identify particular arrangements to be followed in local library settings. The language facilitates the formalization of role expectations and norms in the setting. The meanings of particular events, states of affairs, and personal qualities are altered when they are interpreted in terms of these occupational institutions. The causal and moral texture of the institutions of librarianship gives a sense of purpose and consequence to activities. Those familiar with the standards and principles of librarianship acknowledge a distinct hierarchy of occupational authority and responsibility centering on the professional librarian. Those who recognize the relevance of these standards and principles, and yet are unfamiliar with their specifics, defer to the judgment of librarians. These processes contribute to the legitimacy and power of the professional librarian and are activated in settings collectively oriented toward the library associations representing their interests.

Occupational authority is a function of the normative foundations established by library associations and schools outside the work setting and collective normative orientations toward the occupation within the work setting. The status of the librarian depends on the collective orientations of others. Nonlibrarians as well as librarians must acknowledge, collectively, the relevance of the standards of library service and librarianship to the operation of the library. In occupationally oriented work settings status expectations corresponded to the occupational status order prescribed by library associations. These status expectations create within each setting an interpersonal source of power for librarians. In settings collectively oriented toward the librarian occupation that power is legitimized by the institutions of librarianship. Nonlibrarians tend to comply with work practices that reflect occupational standards. Librarians tend to use their power to establish procedures that comply with those standards.

Appendix A
Research Procedures

Sampling Procedures

A cross-sectional survey of library work settings was mounted in the summer of 1974 to assess the impact of occupational institutions on organizational work arrangements. A directory of libraries, prepared by the Government of Alberta, was used to obtain a preliminary estimate of the population of libraries with four or more full-time positions within the province (Church, 1972). This list was amended to include other libraries suggested by librarians at eight libraries (including an archive as well as university, college, public, government, and business libraries). Where these informants were not certain that a library had four full-time positions, a long distance telephone call was placed to determine its size. It seems relatively certain that a complete enumeration of the population was attained. An attempt was made to sample 94.4 percent (34 of 36) of the population; contact was established with 91.7 percent (33 of 36) of the population; the interview was completed with 88.9 percent (32 of 36) of the population (a mortality rate of 3 percent—1 of 33). In six cases the work setting constituted one department within a larger library. In another four cases the setting corresponded to an autonomous library division within a university library system (the educational curriculum and instruction materials centers and the medical library divisions at two universities). In the twenty-two remaining cases the work setting included all the personnel working in the library. The thirty-two settings included in the survey coincided with the entire library in most cases.

Defining the Tasks and the Work Setting

The unit of analysis was defined as the setting in which two activities—reference and selection of new materials—were performed. Defining the unit in terms of two concrete tasks restricted the survey to one industry, to organizations variously called libraries, learning resource centers, material centers, and archives. There were at least two advantages associated with this procedure. First, making most of the items in the survey instrument specific to the task or the situation, the data would more accurately represent the detailed, contingent nature of the norms in each setting. At the same time the likelihood was increased that data obtained on one of the settings would be comparable to data gained on the others. Second, limiting the survey to one type of industry reduced the number of factors that would have to be estimated and statistically controlled.

The work setting demarcated by reference and selection activities possesses an integrity that made sampling a practical possibility. Both tasks command a considerable proportion of the time and attention of those who perform them. This and the regularity with which they are performed make it possible to designate the bounds of the unit of analysis in terms of the times, places, and people involved in the performance of these two activities. Organizational structure represented by reference and selection tasks (the analytic unit of analysis) constituted a socially recognized work setting within libraries.

Organizational structure at the technical level, its form and degree of formalization, is represented most simply by a pair of tasks. Form is displayed by the division of labor and pattern of interaction between the two activities. Formalization is manifested by the explicitness and consistency of the norms governing task performance. To ensure that size did not restrict the possibilities regarding the division of labor and the pattern of interaction, only those settings with four or more full-time positions were included in the sample.[1]

The descriptions of each task reflected current terminology and behavior in the libraries sampled. During the course of preliminary work in the field, I familiarized myself with the administrative structure of a university library, studying charts that diagramed the flow of operations in various sectors of the library and observing the actual performance of some of the tasks identified on those charts. This investigation suggested that reference work and the judgmental aspects of selecting materials for acquisition might be suitable tasks. Informal contact was extended to include three additional libraries: a library within a large business corporation, a department of the central branch of a public library system, and a learning resources center in a community college. Discussions with those in charge of work settings in each library yielded detailed, step-by-step accounts of the actions involved in the completion of each task. The high level of agreement from one library to the next on the actions and sequences of each task indicated that these activities had meanings that were consistent across different settings. The common actions and sequences identified with each task were drafted as standardized definitions. These definitions were presented on the cover sheet of the survey instrument and provided the basis for initial discussion.

The respondents in the work settings demonstrated a capacity to translate these standardized definitions into concrete and precise boundaries. On the basis of the descriptions provided on the cover sheet, respondents were asked at first to list the names of everyone who provided reference service, even if they did so on a very irregular basis. This question was repeated to identify those who had selected new materials. After classifying those named according to their occupational status, they were asked to check those people who provided reference service or selected new materials in the past week. Having a list of the names of the people who actually did those activities in their setting in addition to the standardized definitions, they were then able to answer relatively detailed questions about those activities. At the same time, the respondents generated concrete representations of the bounds of their work setting and revealed whether the standardized definitions were problematic.

The survey instrument was pretested in seven libraries—in the business, community college, and public libraries contacted earlier as well as in four other libraries. In each setting respondents treated the problem of naming the actual performers of each activity as a factual problem. Reiteration of the definitions satisfied the queries that were raised. They were far more troubled by the accuracy of their reports than by the actual meaning of the tasks as defined. The reactions of the respondents during the pretest indicated that, for all practical purposes, the unit of analysis was recognized as a social setting, that the bounds of that setting could be agreed on, and that the tasks used to define that unit had a relatively invariant meaning from one setting to another.

Senior administrators appeared to also recognize the integrity of the work settings as defined in terms of reference and selection. Where library operations were subdivided into specialized departments, each department carried out both reference and selection activities within its area of responsibility. Where a departmental structure existed, respondents identified the bounds of their work setting as coterminous with the limits of their department.[2]

Specification of the unit of analysis had implications for almost every aspect of the research design. The standardized definitions of the tasks used to denote the unit made a survey possible. Data obtained in different organizations could be compared. That these tasks could be identified as a work setting delimited in terms of particular personnel, times, and locations meant that the unit was not entirely an analytic entity. Both the researcher and the respondents could recognize the unit of analysis. The organizational structure and occupational orientations of the unit of analysis could be measured in a more straightforward fashion. Instead of questioning individual respondents about their personal characteristics and then aggregating their responses to get collective properties, I asked respondents to report directly the collective properties of their work setting. The capacity to couch questions about structure and orientations in task-specific or situation-specific terms further enhanced the validity of the measurement procedures. The care devoted to defining the unit of analysis was expected to increase the interpretability of the data produced by the survey.

Notes

1. The School Library Manpower Task Analysis Survey ["School library personnel task analysis survey," *American Libraries* 1(1970): 177] found that market differentiation of tasks was not evident until staff size reached a certain level—in that case, three or more persons.

2. This condition was violated in one of the thirty-three settings contacted. The interview in this case was broken off by the interviewer as a result of the

querulous and seemingly uncooperative stance of the person in charge of the library department. In retrospect, it seems likely that the unit of analysis as defined analytically did not correspond to the social boundaries of the department. This library was departmentalized in such a way that the selection of new materials was assigned to one department and reference services to another. The questions in the survey presumed that these two activities were performed within the one work setting. For this reason the questions in the interview may have seemed unnatural or unrealistic to the respondents.

Appendix B
Organizational Factors Unrelated to Occupational Work Arrangements

Organizations often rely on other organizations as sources of qualified personnel rather than training their own. Use of trained labor, preprocessed materials, developed land or capital, or credit resources may indicate the existence of a system of interdependent, specialized organizations. Organizational specialization would be reflected in complementary patterns of supplying goods or services. Many organizations provide only some of the goods or services requested by their clients, systemically relying on other organizations to satisfy the balance. The focus here is on dependency relations that might link one library to another, forming library systems. Specifically, the sources of labor, interlibrary contacts, and the patterns of library use were studied to determine whether different library settings operated within common environments.

Sources of Personnel

The settings apparently did not compete with one another for personnel. Of the individuals interviewed in the survey, about one-quarter had no previous job experience. Among those who did have prior experience, over three-quarters of them (52 of 68) had been employed in libraries outside the province or in libraries with fewer than four positions (by libraries not in the sample). In most instances the library settings do not draw on each other for personnel. This was especially true for nonprofessional staff. Those in charge of each setting confirmed that assistants and clerks were hired locally. No distinct market existed for their types of skills. However, by virtue of being certified by schools of library science, a distinct labor market existed for librarians.

Of the ninety-two people who were interviewed, fifty-six (60.9 percent) had received university-level training for work in libraries. Of those who had received training, over one-quarter (16 of 56) had gone to school within the province, at the University of Alberta. However, the tendency to draw trained personnel from a common source was not great. The number who reported being trained in other Canadian, out-of-province schools was greater than the number trained within the province (20 versus 16). An equal number (20) received their training abroad, no two of them from the same school. The lack of structure in the labor market may be due to the rapid expansion in the number and size of libraries in the province since World War II.

Interlibrary Contacts

In over half of the settings, respondents reported that during the year they had contacted from six to thirteen other libraries in the course of providing reference service or selecting materials for acquisition. An inspection of these contacts did not reveal any clear patterns of bilaterial or hierarchical dependencies. Library systems would exist if interlibrary loans and consultation reduced the necessity for all libraries to have more complete collections of material. In order to supplement their own specialized collection, peripheral libraries are allowed to draw on the more complete holdings of central libraries. Had any patterns of bilateral or hierarchical dependencies been detected, the dependencies might have been due to the integration of the internal operations of several libraries into a single interconnected system of libraries.

Patterns of Library Use

The apparent absence of any library systems was supported by the fact that each library setting appeared to serve different and geographically distinct sets of users. When questioned about the other libraries that their clientele might use, most librarians seemed to be hard pressed to suggest possibilities. They frequently countered that almost all requests were handled without referring users to other libraries. Specialized collections seemed to reduce the choice available to library users rather than increasing interlibrary interdependence.

The thirty-two settings seemed to operate within different, basically non-overlapping contexts. They catered to different, often geographically separated sets of clientele. Most settings drew their staff, both trained and untrained, from quite divergent sources. No center-periphery pattern of interlibrary contacts could be discerned. It seems that each library setting operated as an autonomous unit, relatively independent from the others.

Bibliography

"Accreditation of programs of education for librarianship." 1970. *American Libraries* 1:62-65.

"Accreditation—Pro and Con." 1975. *Feliciter* 215:10-12.

"ALA goals and objectives, revised draft." 1975. *American Libraries* 6:39-41.

Aiken, J., and M. Hage. 1969. "Routine technology, social structure, and organizational goals." *Administrative Science Quarterly* 14:366-376.

Aldrich, H.E., and J. Pfeffer. 1976. "Environments of organizations." *Annual Review of Sociology* 2:79-105.

Angel, M.R., and G.R. Brown. 1976. "Survey of library technician programs in Canada." *Canadian Library Journal* 34:41-55.

Asch, S.E. 1958. "Effects of group pressure upon the modification and distortion of judgments." In E.E. Maccoby, T.M. Newcomb, and E.L. Hartley, eds., *Readings in Social Psychology*, 3d ed., pp. 171-183. New York: Holt, Rinehart and Winston.

Asheim, L. 1968. "Education and manpower for librarianship." *American Library Association Bulletin*, 1096-2006.

_____ . 1971. "I'm glad you asked that." *American Libraries* 2:597-599.

Atkinson, P., M. Reid, and P. Sheldrake. 1977. "Medical mystique." *Sociology of Work and Occupations* 4:243-280.

Becker, H.S., and B. Geer. 1958. "The fate of idealism in medical school." *American Sociological Review* 23:50-56.

Berger, P.L., and T. Luckmam. 1966. *The Social Construction of Reality*. New York: Doubleday.

Biblartz, D., M. Capron, L. Kennedy, J. Ross, and D. Weinertn. 1975. "Professional associations and unions: Future impact for today's decisions." *College and Research Libraries* 36:121-128.

Bishop, O.B. 1973. *The Use of Professional Staff in Libraries: A Review, 1923-1971*. CLA Occasional Paper No. 81. Ottawa: Canadian Library Association.

Bissell, C.T. 1974. "Reactions to 'Accreditation—There are choices.'" *Canadian Library Journal* 31 2:122-124.

Blau, P.M. 1968. "The hierarchy of authority in organizations." *American Journal of Sociology* 73:453-467.

Blau, P.M., W.V. Heydebrand, and R.E. Stauffer. 1966. "The structure of small bureaucracies." *American Sociological Review* 31:179-191.

Blau, P.M., and W.R. Scott. 1962. *Formal Organizations*. San Francisco: Chandler.

Boissonas, C. 1972. "ALA and professionalism." *American Libraries* 3:972-979.

Canadian Library Association Council. 1947. *Conference Proceedings*. Ottawa: Canadian Library Association.

"Canadian library technicians." 1974. *Feliciter* 20:8.

Child, J. 1972. "Organizational structure and strategies of control: A replication of the Aston Study." *Administrative Science Quarterly* 17:163-177.

Christianson, E. 1973. *Paraprofessional and Nonprofessional Staff in Special Libraries*. SLA State-of-the-Art Review No. 2. New York: Special Libraries Association.

Church, L. 1972. *A Directory of Libraries in Alberta, 1972*. Edmonton, Alberta: Department of Culture, Youth and Recreation, Province of Alberta.

Cicourel, A.V., and J.I. Kitsuse. 1963. *The Educational Decisionmakers*. New York: Bobbs-Merrill.

Clark, B.R. 1972. "The organizational sage in higher education." *Administrative Science Quarterly* 17 2:178-184.

Cloward, R.A. 1959. "Illegitimate means, anomie, and deviant behavior." *American Sociological Review* 24:164-176.

"CLTA (Canadian Library Technicians Association) executive meets in Thunder Bay." 1972. *Ontario Library Review*, June, p. 121.

Converse, P., and A. Campbell. 1960. "Political standards in secondary groups." In D. Cartwright and A. Zander, eds, *Group Dynamics: Research and Theory*, 2d ed., pp. 300-318. New York: Harper and Row.

"Criteria for programs to prepare library media technical assistants." 1971. *American Libraries* 2:1059-1063.

"Collective bargaining for librarians." 1974. *CAUT Bulletin* 23:4.

Dalton, M. 1959. *Men Who Manage*. New York: John Wiley and Sons.

Descriptive List of Professional and Nonprofessional Duties in Libraries. 1948. Chicago: American Library Association.

Dornbusch, S.M., and W.R. Scott. 1975. *Evaluation and the Exercise of Authority*. San Francisco: Jossey-Bass.

Duncan, C.D. 1966. "Path analysis: Sociological examples." *American Journal of Sociology* 72:1-16.

Ellsworth, R.C. 1973. "The library technician: An emerging Canadian profile." *Libri* 23:122-128.

Etzioni, A. 1964. *Modern Organizations* Englewood Cliffs, N.J.: Prentice-Hall, Inc.

"Fanshawe College replies to the 'Summary of a survey of library technician training programs in Alberta, British Columbia, Manitoba, Ontario, Quebec and Saskatchewan.'" 1973. *Feliciter* January 19, pp. 5-6.

Friedson, E. 1970. *Professional Dominance*. New York: Atherton Press.

———. 1973. "Professionalization and the organization of middle-class labor in postindustrial society." In P. Halmos, ed., *Professionalization and Social Change*, pp. 47-59. Sociological Review Monograph 20.

Galbraith, J.K. 1971. *The New Industrial State*, 2d. ed. Boston: Houghton Mifflin Company.

Garfinkel, H. 1964. "Studies of the routine grounds of everyday activities." *Social Problems* 11:225-250.

Goldberg, A.I. 1976. "The relevance of cosmopolitan/local orientations to professional values and behavior." *Sociology of Work and Occupations* 3:331-356.

Goldner, F.H., and R.R. Ritti. 1967. "Professionalization as career immobility." *American Journal of Sociology* 72:489-502.

Goode, W.J. 1957. "Community within a community: The professions." *American Sociological Review* 22:194-200.

____ . 1961. "The librarian: From occupation to profession?" *Library Quarterly* 31:306-320.

____ . 1969. "The theoretical limits of professionalization." In A. Etzioni, ed., *The Semi-Professions and Their Organization*, pp. 266-315. New York: Free Press.

"Graduate library school programs accredited by the American Library Association." 1971. *American Libraries* 2:1091-1092.

"Guidelines for using volunteers in Libraries." 1971. *American Libraries* 2:407-408.

Gwinup, T. 1974. "The failure of librarians to attain profession." *Wilson Library Bulletin* 48:482-490.

Hall, R.H. 1963. "The concept of bureaucracy: An empirical assessment." *American Journal of Sociology* 69:32-40.

____ .1968. "Professionalization and bureaucratization." *American Sociological Review* 33:92-104.

____ . 1969. *Occupations and the Social Structure*. Englewood Cliffs, N.J.: Prentice-Hall.

Heydebrand, W.V. 1973. "Autonomy, complexity, and non-bureaucratic coordination in professional organizations." In W.V. Heydebrand, ed., *Comparative Organizations: The Results of Empirical Research*, pp. 158-188. Englewood Cliffs, N.J.: Prentice-Hall.

Hickson, J.J., and M.W. Thomas. 1969. "Professionalization in Britain: A preliminary measurement." *Sociology* 3:37-53.

Homans, G.C. 1950. *The Human Group*. New York: Harcourt, Brace and World, Inc.

Hughes, E.C. 1958. *Men and Their Work*. Glencoe, Ill.: Free Press.

Inkson, J.H.R., D.S. Pugh, and D.J. Hickson. 1970. "Organizational context and structure: An abbreviated replication." *Administrative Science Quarterly* 15:318-329.

Johnson, T.J. 1972. *Professions and Power*. London: MacMillan.

Kaplan, N. 1965. "Professional scientists in industry: A critical essay." *Social Problems* 13:88-97.

Katz, E., and S.N. Eisenstadt. 1960. "Bureaucracy and its clientele: A case study." *Administrative Science Quarterly* 5:253-271.

Knapp, P.B. 1973. "The library as a complex organization: Implications for library education." In C. Rawski, ed., *Toward A Theory of Librarianship*, pp. 473-494. Metuehen, N.J.: Scarecrow.

Kronus, C.L. 1976a. "The evolution of occupational power." *Sociology of Work and Occupations* 3:3-37.

_____ .1976b. "Occupational versus organizational influences on reference group identification." *Sociology of Work and Occupations* 3:303-330.

Lehman, E.W. 1969. "Toward a macrosociology of power." *American Sociological Review* 34:453-464.

"Library bill of rights revision." 1979. *American Libraries* 10:208.

"Library education and manpower." 1970. *American Libraries* 1:341-344, 665.

Logsdon, R.H. 1970. "The librarian and the scholar: Eternal enemies." *Library Journal* 95:2871-2874.

Mann, M. 1973. *Consciousness and Action among the Western Working Class.* London: MacMillan.

Mannheim, K. 1960. *Man and Society in an Age of Reconstruction.* London: K. Paul, Trench, Trubner and Company.

Marshall, J. 1970. "The occupational content." In A. Campbell and I. Dawson eds., *The Library Technician at Work: Theory and Practice.* Proceedings of a Workshop held at Lakehead University, Canadian Library Association. Thunder Bay: Lakehead University.

Marshall, J.M. and J.E. Munroe. 1971. *Summary of a Survey of Library Technician Programs in Alberta, British Columbia, Manitoba, Ontario, and Saskatchewan*, 3d rev. ed. Committee on the Training of Library Technicians. Ottawa: Canadian Library Association.

_____ . 1972. "Summary of a survey of library technician training programs in Alberta, British Columbia, Manitoba, Ontario, Quebec and Saskatchewan." *Feliciter* 18 7:3-16.

McHugh, P. 1968. *Defining the Situation.* New York: Bobbs-Merrill.

Megrian, L.D. 1974. "Library education in the higher education systems of Australia and Canada, 1960, 1970." *Libri* 24:61-68.

Merton, R. 1957. "The role-set: Problems in sociological theory." *British Journal of Sociology* 8:110-120.

Merton, R. 1952. "Bureaucratic structure and personality." In R.K. Merton, A.P. Gray, B. Hockey, and H.C. Selvin, eds., *Reader in Bureaucracy*, pp. 361-371. Glencoe, Ill.: Free Press.

Meyer, John W., and Brian Rowan. 1977. "Institutionalized organizations: Formal structure as myth and ceremony." *American Journal of Sociology* 83:340-363.

Mueller, J.H., K.F. Schuessler, and H.L. Costner. 1977. *Statistical Reasoning in Sociology* (third edition). Boston: Houghton Mifflin Company.

Milgram, S. 1965. "Some conditions of obedience and disobedience to authority." *Human Relations* 18:57-76.

"MLS evaluation at the University of Alberta." 1978. *Feliciter* 24:4.

"New standards of accreditation." 1972. *American Libraries* 3:882.

North, J. 1976. "Librarianship: A profession?" *Canadian Library Journal* 34:253-257.

Orne, M.T., and F.J. Evans. 1965. "Social control in the psychological experiment: Antisocial behavior and hypnosis." *Journal of Personality and Social Psychology* 1:189-200.

Pantazis, F. 1977. "Library technicians in Ontario academic libraries." *Canadian Library Journal* 35:77-91.

Parsons, T. 1947. *Max Weber: The Theory of Social and Economic Organization* Edited by T. Parsons, translated by A.M. Henderson and T. Parsons. New York: The Free Press.

_____. 1960. "Some ingredients of a general theory of formal organization." In *Structure and Process in Modern Society*. Glencoe, Ill. Free Press.

Pennings, J. 1973. "Measures of organizational structure." *American Journal of Sociology* 79:686-704.

Perrow, C. 1979. *Complex Organizations: A Critical Essay*. Glenview, Ill.: Scott, Foresman, and Company.

Pfeffer, J. 1974. "Administrative regulations and licensing: Social problem or solution?" *Social Problems* 21:468-479.

Position Classification and Principles of Academic Status in Canadian University Libraries. 1969. Canadian Association of College and University Libraries. Ottawa: Canadian Library Association.

Professional and Non-Professional Duties in Libraries. 1963. London: Library Association.

_____. 1974. London: Library Association.

Price, J.L. 1972. *Handbook of Organizational Measurement*. Lexington, Mass.: D.C. Heath and Company.

"Proposed standards for accreditation, 1972." 1972. *American Libraries* 3:653-657.

Roth, J.A. 1974. "Professionalism: The sociologist's decoy." *Sociology of Work and Occupations* 1:6-23.

Rothenberg, L.B., J. Lucianovic, D.A. Kronick, and A.M. Rees. 1971. "A job-task index for evaluating professional utilization in libraries." *Library Quarterly* 41 4:320-328.

Rothstein, S. 1974. "A tale of two associations, CLA and ALA; Considering Canadian library school accreditation." *Canadian Library Journal* 31:76-78.

Rushing, W.A. 1964. *The Psychiatric Professions*. Chapel Hill, N.C.: University of North Carolina Press.

Schroeder, J. 1975. "The bargaining unit for the academic librarian." *Canadian Library Journal* 32:463-473.

Scott, W.R. 1965. "Reactions to supervision in a heteronomous organization." *Administrative Science Quarterly* 20:65-81.

———. 1966. "Professionals in bureaucracies." In H.M. Vollmer and D.L. Mills, eds., *Professionalization*, pp. 265-275. Englewood Cliffs, N.J. Prentice-Hall.

———. 1970. *Social Processes and Social Structures*. New York: Holt, Rinehart, and Winston.

Scott, W.R., S.M. Dornbusch, B.C. Busching, and J.D. Laing. 1967. "Organizational evaluation and authority." *Administrative Science Quarterly* 12:93-105.

Selznick, P. 1949. *TVA and the Grass Roots*. Berkeley and Los Angeles: University of California Press.

Shaffer, D.E. 1968. *The Maturity of Librarianship as a Profession*. Metuchen, N.J.: Scarecrow Press.

Simon, H.A. 1957. *Administrative Behavior*. London: Collier-MacMillan.

Simpson, R.L., and I.H. Simpson. 1969. "Women and bureaucracy in the semi-professions." In A. Etzioni, ed., *The Semi-Professions and Their Organization*, pp. 197-265. New York: Free Press.

"Special report on librarians." 1965. *CAUT Bulletin* 24 5:12-22.

Starbuck, W. 1976. "The organization and its environment." In M. Dunnette, ed., *Handbook of Industrial and Organizational Psychology*. Chicago: Rand, McNally.

"Statement on accreditation and the employment situation." 1975. *American Libraries* 6:39.

Stinchcombe, A.L. 1959. "Bureaucratic and craft administration of production: A comparative study." *Administrative Science Quarterly* 4:168-187.

———. 1965. "Social structure and organizations." In J.G. March, ed., *Handbook of Organizations*, pp. 142-193 Chicago: Rand McNally.

Stone, D. 1974. "The prospects of unionism." *American Libraries* 5:364-366.

Summers, F.W., and R.E. Bidlack. 1972. "New standards for accreditation." *American Libraries* 3:658-660.

Thompson, J.D. 1967. *Organizations in Action*. New York: McGraw-Hill.

Thompson, J.D., and W.J. McEwan. 1958. "Organizational goals and environment: Goal-setting as an interaction process." *American Sociological Review* 23:23-31.

Toren, N. 1975. "Deprofessionalization and its sources." *Sociology of Work and Occupations* 2:323-337.

Torrance, E.P. 1954. "Some consequences of power differences on decision making in permanent and temporary three-man groups." *Research Studies* 22:130-140.

Udy, S.H., Jr. 1959. " 'Bureaucracy' and 'Rationality' in Weber's theory: An empirical study." *American Sociological Review* 24:791-795.

Vandergrift, K.E. 1978. "The making of a school librarian." *American Libraries* 9:605-606.

Ward, E. 1974. "The community of interest and academic status." *Canadian Library Journal* 31:540-543.

Weber, M. 1946. *From Max Weber*, Edited and translated by H.H. Gerth and C.W. Mills. New York: Oxford University Press.

    1947. *The Theory of Social and Economic Organization*. New York: Oxford University Press.

Weisenberg, C.C. 1970. "ALA: A professional or a library association?" *American Libraries* 1:1060-1061.

Wilensky, H.L. 1964. "The professionalization of everyone?" *American Journal of Sociology* 70:137-158.

Williams, R.M., Jr. 1960. *American Society*, 2d ed. New York: Knopf.

Woodward, J. 1965. *Industrial Organization: Theory and Practice*. London: Oxford University Press.

Zelditch, M., Jr. 1962. "Can you really study an army in the laboratory?" In A. Etzioni, ed., *A Sociological Reader on Complex Organizations*, 2d ed., pp. 528-539. New York: Holt, Rinehart and Winston.

———. 1969. "Some methodological problems of field studies." In G.J. McCall and J.L. Simmons, eds., pp. 5-19 *Issues in Participant Observation*. Reading, Mass.: Addison-Wesley.

Index of Names

159

Index of Subjects

Academic libraries, 56, 67, 102–103, 113–114, 121. *See also* Type of library

Accreditation, 4, 6, 8–9, 26

Acknowledged regulation, 49, 61–64, 71–73; versus official documentation, 62–64, 72–73

Acquisitions budget. *See* Size of the acquisitions budget

Alberta Association of Library Technicians, 38, 43

Associate specialist. *See* Library associate

Authority: amending the conventional perspective, 14–15, 105; conventional perspective, 7, 12, 104–105; demand effects, 134–135; education versus experience, 136; informal control, 109, 111; library association policies, 97–98, 105, 112; occupational and managerial, 109–111, 115–116, 117, 138, 139; organizational factors, 114, 124; pattern of communication, 90–92, 95–96; service deal, 104; status expectations, 132–135

Autonomy of librarians: bureaucratic control, 112–113; spurious interpretations, 103–104, 105; threat to, 102–105; type of library, 67, 96, 121–122

Awareness of library associations. *See* Collective awareness of library associations

Beta, 53

Budget. *See* Size of the acquisitions budget

Bureaucratic control procedures: coherence, 112–114, 125; library association policies, 97–98, 105, 112; managerial versus technical

level, 110; size and, 59–60; versus bureaucratic staff, 111–112. *See also* Job descriptions; Pattern of communication; Written records

Bureaucratization, 109–111

Business libraries, 67, 102–103, 104–105, 113, 114, 121

Career ladder, 18–22

Change, 122–123, 125–126

Causal ordering: in the task domain, 27–30, 89–93; of the theoretical argument, 119, 122–126

Centrality. *See* Type of library

Circulation. *See* Size of circulation

Clientele. *See* Library users; Size of circulation

Code of ethics, 6

Coincidence of values and interests, 36–37; effects suppressed, 65, 70, 120–121; frequency distribution, 37; independent variable, 65, 66, 94, 95, 99; mediates the effects of, 95. *See also* Collective occupational orientation; Collective orientations toward librarians as a status group

Collective awareness of central library associations: effects suppressed, 65, 70, 81, 82, 120–121; frequency distribution, 42; independent variable, 53, 55, 57, 58, 59, 65, 66, 68, 74, 76, 77, 81, 82, 83, 86, 94, 95, 99; mediates the effects of, 74, 77, 95, 101–102, 120–121. *See also* Collective awareness of library associations

Collective awareness of library associations, 36–42, 98–100; versus individual awareness, 38–39. *See also* Collective awareness of central library associations; Collective awareness of specialist associations

About the Author

William Joseph Reeves is currently an assistant professor of sociology at the University of Calgary. Previously, he has worked as a teacher of social studies in Edmonton, Alberta, and as an instructor of political science and economics at the Grande Prairie Junior College in the same province. He received the B.A. in political economy from the University of Alberta, the M.A. in government from Indiana University, and the Ph.D. in sociology from Stanford University.